Establishing Faith

Phase I

Getting Started

Pocket Principles®
and Guided Discussions

For Leaders

NOTE: In an effort to recognize that both men and women are co-heirs of God's grace, we have chosen to use alternating gender pronouns in this document. However, we do recognize and embrace gender-specific roles in Scripture.

Development Team:
Margaret Garner
Jack Larson
Margo Theivagt

Writing Team:
Linda Dukes
Margaret Garner
Jack Larson
Steve Miller
Margo Theivagt

Publishing Team:
Nila Duffitt
Buddy Eades
Margaret Garner
David Parfitt

Design by Cristina van de Hoeve
doodlingdesigner.com

A Welcome from WDA's President
Worldwide Discipleship Association, Inc.

Hello Friend!

Let me congratulate you on your decision to learn more about Jesus Christ and what it means to follow Him. There is nothing more important or more rewarding than the decision to follow Him and then to grow as a Christian.

These studies will help you get started on your journey with Christ or encourage and instruct you if you are already on this exciting journey. We in WDA want to help you grow and become all you can be in Christ Jesus!

Because you have chosen to lead, we want to do all we can to support you. In addition to the materials provided in this workbook, we would like to also offer you a free download of the Teaching Outlines for *Getting Started*. www.disciplebuilding.org/materials/getting-started-teaching-outlines-free-download

My prayer and confident belief is that "he who began a good work in you will carry it on to completion until the day of Christ Jesus" (Philippians 1:6) so that He is able "to present you before his glorious presence without fault and with great joy." (Jude 1:24) To Him be glory and praise!

May God richly bless you as you strive to grow in Him.

Bob Dukes
President, Worldwide Discipleship Association
Fayetteville, GA 30214

Establishing Faith
Table of Contents: Leader

Leader's Instructions
For Using Pocket Principles®

What is a Pocket Principle™? Each Pocket Principle™ is a brief essay that focuses on a single topic necessary to the growth and maturity of a believer.

The 8 Pocket Principles®, about *Getting Started*, are designed to help the new believer begin to get established in his relationship with God or help a more mature believer review important concepts. This material covers topics such as assurance of salvation, baptism, the role of the Holy Spirit, etc.

Using Pocket Principles® In A Guided Discussion (Small Group) Format:

You will notice that each Pocket Principle™ has a corresponding Guided Discussion. Because the students who are studying *Getting Started* are often less mature believers, our suggestion is that they **not be required** to read the Pocket Principles® before coming to the guided discussion or after the discussion. At this point in their maturity, it is best that they not be given work to do outside of the group. (For more information about this, go to our website: www.disciplebuilding.org/about/phases-of-christian-growth/2.) Of course, you can mention the purpose of the Pocket Principles® and **invite** students to read them. They will reinforce truth learned in the group discussion. Also, if a group member misses a meeting, he can read the corresponding Pocket Principle™ to review the information missed.

Using Pocket Principles® In A Life Coaching (One-One) Format:

Pocket Principles® can also be used effectively in an interactive one-one relationship. However, in this arrangement it is suggested that the Life Coach ask the student to read the Pocket Principle™ beforehand so the material can be discussed during the one-one appointment. All the dynamics mentioned above still apply and the Life Coach needs to tailor expectations to the maturity of the student. To facilitate interaction, the material contained in the corresponding Guided Discussion (Leader) will help a Life Coach prepare for the appointment. (For more information about preparing for a Life Coaching appointment, please consult the *Life Coaching Manual* at www.disciplebuilding.org/product-category/life-coaching.)

Leader's Instructions
For Using Guided Discussions

The 8 Guided Discussions, about *Getting Started*, are designed to help the new believer begin to get established in his relationship with God or help a more mature believer review important concepts. This material covers topics such as assurance of salvation, baptism, the role of the Holy Spirit, etc..

Guided Discussions for small groups play an important role in the growth of a believer with the **major goal being interaction around Scripture.** The goal of disciple building is not just knowledge, but Christlikeness in character and conduct. Therefore, **application is essential.** (Sections: "Looking At Real Life" and "Looking at My Life" in the guided discussions are application oriented.) At least one-third of the small group discussion time should be spent discussing application of the truth presented. It is often tempting to get caught up in the content part of the study, but you, as the leader, are responsible to move the group along toward application.

A word needs to be said about the relationship between Pocket Principles® and Guided Discussions. The content of both is generally the same, although not identical. These two (2) formats provide different ways of presenting the same content, or may be used to reinforce the content. (Another type of WDA material is Teaching Outlines. These are designed to be used by a teacher who wants to present the content in a lecture format to a larger group. Free Teaching Outlines can be found at the WDA store on our website at www.disciplebuilding.org/materials/getting-started-teaching-outlines-free-download.)

There are two (2) versions of each study: the Leader's version with answers and special notes, and the Student version with questions, but no answers. *Answers and notes to leaders are in gray, italicized text.*

Much of the preparation has been done for you as a leader: topics have been chosen, Scripture verses selected, questions written. However, it is important that you become comfortable with the material so that you will be able to be flexible and focus on the needs of your group. In the *Small Groups Manual* (WDA), you will find information about the practical aspects of group leadership. Please refer to the section titled "Practical Dynamics of Small Group Leadership." The *Small Groups Manual* is available from the WDA store at www.disciplebuilding.org/store/leadership-manuals/small-groups-manual.

How Can I Be Sure? Part I
Understanding Assurance Of Salvation

INTRODUCTION

Just before leaving on a big trip, I always take a final look around to make sure I've got everything I need. Do I have my wallet, enough money for gas and food, my plane ticket, the papers with the addresses and phone numbers of hotels? Although I'm almost certain I've already put these in the car, I check one last time just to be sure. Why? Because if I've forgotten something essential, I may never make it to my intended destination.

In the same way, after making a decision to follow Christ, I had to look back to make sure I'd done everything right. I knew that if I'd misunderstood some essential aspect of salvation, I might never make it to where I wanted to go—heaven. Because of the importance of this salvation experience, it's only natural that some people question their experience or want to make sure they "did it right." We know that God's done His part in sending His Son to pay for our sins. Our concern is that perhaps we've not done everything right on our part to receive His gracious gift. That's what this lesson is all about.

> Wrong beliefs lead to wrong actions. Having the right belief is critical.

Why not stop reading for a moment and ask God to help you understand His Word on this important topic. If you're not used to talking to God, you could just say something like, *"God, I want to make sure I've done everything I need to do in order to be forgiven and to be Your child. Please help me to understand. Thanks for caring about me!"*

UNDERSTANDING WHAT GOD DID FOR US

First, there are certain things we need to understand and believe. Some people say, "It doesn't matter what you believe, as long as you live consistently with it." Yet, Hitler believed that he was doing the world a favor by killing off "lesser" races and helping the "superior" Aryan race to dominate the earth. Osama Bin Laden believes that Allah wants him to kill people who don't believe as he does. Both Hitler and Bin Laden may have lived consistently with their beliefs. Yet, wrong beliefs lead to wrong actions. Having the right belief is critical. What must we believe to be saved?

The Bad News: We are sinful and this sin separates us from God. Because of our sin, we are lost and can't have a relationship with God through our own efforts.

Imagine that you're in a math class and your teacher says, "You should know how to work all of these problems by now. The passing grade for this pop quiz is 100%." Yet, as you take the test, you realize that you're getting some of the problems wrong. No matter how many you get right from now on, will you ever pass the test? No. Because passing is 100%. No matter how many you get correct from now on, you'll never get 100%. You're gonna fail.

Passing that math test after missing some problems is as impossible as making it to heaven, on our own, after we've already sinned—falling short of God's perfection. Imperfect people can't make it to a perfect heaven on their own merits. This is the first thing we need to believe.

The Good News: Knowing that we couldn't save ourselves, God sent His Son Jesus Christ to save us. Jesus lived a perfect, sinless life in obedience to His heavenly Father. When He died on the cross, He wasn't dying for His own sins, but for our sins. He paid the penalty that we deserved to pay.

> When Jesus died on the cross, He wasn't dying for His own sins, but for our sins.

For Christ died for sins once for all, the righteous for the unrighteous, to bring you to God. (I Peter 3:18a)

But God demonstrates His own love for us in this: While we were still sinners, Christ died for us. (Romans 5:8)

Imagine that last year you found a misplaced folder at work that proved your employers were exaggerating their profits to make their company look good to the stock holders. Although you knew you should go public with the information, you thought of your responsibility to your family and didn't want to risk getting fired. Now you sit in a courtroom before a judge who finds you guilty of participating in the crime by withholding information. He says that you must either pay a fine of $100,000.00 or serve 10 years in jail. You tell him you don't have $100,000.00. As a righteous judge, he declares you guilty.

Then the judge, seeing the distress on your face and the faces of your children, appears to be holding back tears as he writes something that only he can see. He hands it to a courtroom aid, who delivers it to you. You gasp as you realize that the judge has just written you a check for $100,000.00, offering to pay the entire penalty that you owed.

That's what the Bible calls grace—God offering a payment for what you owed, not because you deserved it, but because of His great love. How astounding that God would pay our debt with the sacrifice of His Son!

But it's not enough for God to offer this gift. You could reject the check offered to you by the gracious judge. How do we receive God's grace? It's not enough to believe in God and believe that Jesus died for our sins. According to the Bible, even demons believe in God (James 2:19). We must receive His forgiveness through repentance and faith. Let's look at these one at a time.

RESPONDING THE WAY GOD WANTS US TO RESPOND

Repent From Our Sins. Repentance is our response to the bad news: our sinfulness and rebellion against God. The simplest definition of repentance is "a willingness to change." Don't get confused here! We're not saying that we change so that God will save us. That would be salvation by works! Besides, we can't make a lot of changes in our lives until God renews us and empowers us to live a new life. We're simply saying that we make a mental change of allegiance, from bowing to self to bowing to God. In repentance we tell God, "I'm willing to change! I want to turn from my sin and serve You!"

From that time on Jesus began to preach, 'Repent, for the kingdom of heaven is near.' (Matthew 4:17)

Believe In Jesus. Faith or belief in Christ is our appropriate response to the good news.

For it is by grace you have been saved, through faith—and this not from yourselves, it is the gift of God—not by works, so that no one can boast. (Ephesians 2:8,9)

For God so loved the world that He gave His one and only Son, that whoever believes in Him shall not perish but have eternal life. (John 3:16)

It's more than saying mentally, "I believe Jesus existed and worked miracles and rose from the dead." To believe in Jesus means that you put your trust in Him. It's like people who say that they believe in aerobic exercise. They don't mean merely that they believe that somewhere in the world, aerobic exercise classes exist. They mean that they believe enough in aerobics to be willing to do aerobics. If a person says she believes in Coke, she's saying more than she believes Coca-Cola exists. She believes in it enough as a refreshing beverage that she's willing to drink it.

> In repentance we tell God, "I'm willing to change! I want to turn from my sin and serve you!"

Similarly, faith in Christ is more than an intellectual agreement that He exists. It's putting our trust in Him to save us. It's entrusting ourselves to Him. We're saying that we believe that God has offered us forgiveness through the death of Christ for our sins and we accept the payment that He offers. We're also saying that we're willing to follow Christ.

PUTTING IT ALL TOGETHER

Although repentance and faith focus on two different things, sin and Christ, they are actually one mental act. As we turn away from our sin, we turn toward Christ at the same time. As Jesus said,

'The time has come,' he said. 'The kingdom of God is near. Repent and believe the good news!' (Mark 1:15)

Although repentance and faith focus on two different things, sin and Christ, they are actually one mental act.

So, let's go back to the important trip we talked about at the beginning of this lesson. In order to make sure I could make it to my destination, I asked myself, "Did I bring my plane ticket? Did I bring enough cash?" In the same way, if we want to make sure that we are truly God's children and are going to make it to heaven, we must ask, "Have I truly repented of my sins? Have I truly believed on Jesus?" If you know that you haven't, or if you're simply not sure, why not confirm your decision by expressing it to God in prayer. He's not so interested in the words you use as He is the sincerity of your heart. If this written prayer expresses the desire of your heart, why not say it to God right now?

"God, I've gone my own way. I'm sorry. I'm turning from my sins. Give me the strength to follow You. I believe in You, putting my trust in you to save me from my sins. Make me into a new person and take me to heaven. Thanks for forgiving me and loving me so much!"

If you prayed that prayer and sincerely meant it, then on the authority of God's Word, you are His child and you are successfully headed to your destination—heaven!

FACTS VERSUS FEELINGS

You're having one of those days. You didn't get enough sleep last night. Your boss treats you like dirt. You go to your home fellowship meeting and hope to get some encouragement. Instead, you see this bubbly Christian who never seems down who tells about how God solved all her problems. "All my problems aren't solved," you think. Then a new Christian gives a dramatic testimony about how he received Christ and felt something like electricity go through his entire body. "I didn't have a big emotional experience when I got saved," you think. Then you begin to wonder if you're really a Christian at all.

This is where you must put emotions in their place. The Bible said, *"whoever believes in Him shall not perish but have eternal life." (John 3:16)* It didn't say, "whoever feels bubbly all the time" will have eternal life. It didn't say, "whoever has a dramatic emotional experience" will have eternal life. It says that *"whoever believes in Him shall…have eternal life."*

So, if I truly believe/repent, but am not saved, what would this say about God? (He would be a liar. And if God's a liar, we're all up the creek!) So the salvation of those who repent and believe is as secure as the promise of God, regardless of how we feel.

Hint: Some people offset future doubts by writing down exactly what they understood and prayed when they received Christ. For example, you might photocopy this lesson and write at the end, "I understood this lesson and prayed this prayer for assurance of my salvation on this day" (write out date). Next, put it in a safe place.

Ten years from now, when you have another one of those bad days and Satan whispers in your ear, "You didn't know what you were doing when you prayed that prayer ten years ago," you can take it out and show Satan exactly what you did. Your salvation is as secure as the promise of God. Then you can tell Satan to "get lost."

How Can I Be Sure? Part I
Understanding Assurance Of Salvation

Important to Leader: *Answers and notes to leaders are in gray, italicized text.*

GOAL:

For the disciple to be sure that he understands the Gospel and to determine if he has or has not committed his life to Christ.

GETTING STARTED:

When you leave on a family vacation you may have a list of everything the family will need. What are some of the things you must have (or must have done) to have a good vacation?

Money, credit cards, luggage, gear for the location and activities, prescriptions, snacks, maps, appropriate clothes, games, have car checked over and fuelled, arrange for pets to be cared for, for the mail to be dealt with, etc.

Transition: *In a similar way, a new believer needs to be sure he has done everything necessary for beginning his relationship with Jesus. So, let's talk about what is involved in becoming a Christian.*

STUDYING TOGETHER:

The Gospel that explains how to become a Christian has 3 parts: the Bad News, the Good News, and Man's Response.

BAD NEWS

Read Romans 3:9-18,23.

1. In these verses Paul describes the condition of all people who are not Christians. Describe that condition.

    Everyone without Christ is sinful, and cannot come into the presence of God, and really doesn't want to be in His presence. They cannot please Him, are lost and cannot find God (are separated from God).

2. What do you think sin is?

After listening to group members' answers, summarize being sure to communicate that sin is falling short of God's perfection. Another way to put it is rebellion against God, passive indifference to God.

Read Romans 3:19-20.

3. How does God let us know we are sinful?

He tells us in His Word.

GOOD NEWS

Read I Peter 3:18a.

4. What is the Good News?

God provided a way back into relationship with Him through Jesus Christ's death for our sins. On our own, there is no way we could have restored our relationship with God.

MAN'S RESPONSE

Even though God has provided a way for people to come back into a relationship with him, it is necessary for a person to receive the gift of salvation. An illustration of this: A man was on death row, and at the last moment was granted a pardon by the Governor. When told about this, the prisoner said, "Thanks but no thanks." The State Supreme court ruled that a pardon can be granted, but is not effective unless the pardon is accepted. The man was put to death.

We must receive the pardon that God has offered us. Scripture uses two words (repentance and faith) to describe what is required in order to receive salvation (the pardon God has offered).

REPENTANCE

Read Acts 3:19.

5. What does the word "repentance" mean?

    After students give their answers, present the following:

    Repentance—"a willingness to change."
    O.T.: shubv: means "to turn away from sin and toward God"
    N.T.: metanoeo: means "to change one's mind," in this case, about sin.

6. Some people think that "metanoeo" means to change your life. Explain why this is incorrect.

    It is incorrect because without the help of God we don't have the power to change our lives. All we can do is have a willingness to change. And then if we are willing, God will supply the power to change our life.

FAITH IN CHRIST

Read John 3:16.

7. What does faith in Christ mean?

    Trusting Him alone for salvation (not just a mental assent to who He is) and being willing to follow Him.

8. Some people think that faith means to obey Christ. Why is this incorrect?

    Faith means a willingness to follow Christ, not the ability to obey apart from the power of God.

    Summary: *Repentance from sin means a willingness to change. Salvation comes about when I'm willing to change my direction in life (repent) and follow Christ (faith).*

LOOKING AT REAL LIFE:

9. What are some of the reasons people give for not becoming a Christian?

   I'll do it later, I don't believe in God, I'm as good as anyone else, I'm a good person, a loving God won't send me to hell. I've gone to church all my life.

10. What would you say to a person who said, "I was raised in the church so I'm a Christian"?

    All of us are born separated from God and until we repent and put our faith in Christ, we aren't Christians. Going to church doesn't guarantee that a person has come to the point of repentance and faith.

11. What would you say to a person who said, "My life is as good as anyone else's, so I'll go to heaven"?

    Everyone has sinned and no one is good enough on his own to go to heaven. Our problem with sin must be dealt with before we can have a relationship with a holy God. God has made it possible for us to have a relationship with Him by sending Jesus to die for us. So we must accept that as the sacrifice for our sin. We must repent and have faith in Christ.

LOOKING AT MY LIFE:

Why would you say that you are a Christian, or not a Christian, based on the information in this lesson?

If you have made this decision for Christ, write a letter of gratitude to God.

If you have not yet made this decision for Christ, write a letter telling God where you are in the process.

How Can I Be Sure? Part II
Prescription For Doubters

INTRODUCTION

I heard about a man who wanted to travel by ship from America to Europe, but could scrape together only enough money for a ticket, thus having no money to purchase food at the ship's restaurant. So, he packed his own cheese and crackers, avoiding the restaurant, where people feasted daily on the most delicious foods.

Days later, as the crackers went stale and the cheese was probably beginning to mold, a fellow passenger pulled the wretched man aside and inquired, "I noticed that you never dine with us in the cafeteria. Would you mind telling me why?" He confessed his inability to pay for anything except for the ticket, to which his new acquaintance replied, "But didn't you understand? The food came with the ticket!"[1]

> As a "new creation," we have a fresh, new relationship with God and the desire to pursue that relationship.

Tragically, many Christians are just like this man. They never grew enough spiritually to understand all that came with their ticket to heaven. Existing on spiritual cheese and crackers, they miss the spiritual feast that God says comes with salvation. Today let's begin to look at a few items in the feast, and the doubts that keep some from enjoying that feast.

PRESENT DECLARATIONS

Salvation isn't just about life after death. We possess eternal life here and now, along with its many benefits. Here are just a few:

Forgiveness. Some Christians continue to go to bed at night, racked with guilt for their past behavior. Yet, from God's perspective, those sins are gone, taken away as far as the East is from the West, flung into the deepest sea. We no longer have to be shackled by guilt! As concentration camp survivor Corrie ten Boom put it, "When we confess our sins, God casts them into the deepest ocean, gone forever. And even though I cannot find a Scripture for it, I believe God then places a sign out there that says, NO FISHING ALLOWED."[2]

In Him we have redemption through His blood, the forgiveness of sins, in accordance with the riches of God's grace.... (Ephesians 1:7)

A New Creation. Some people think, "I've made such a mess of my life that it would be better if I started over from scratch." That's why God did more than simply help us rehabilitate our old lives. He started off fresh, giving us a new birth into His family. As a "new creation," we have a fresh, new relationship with God and the desire to pursue that relationship.

Therefore, if anyone is in Christ, the new creation has come: The old has gone, the new is here! (II Corinthians 5:17)

The Holy Spirit. God didn't save us and then leave us to live the rest of our lives in our own power. At our salvation, His Spirit comes to live inside of us, offering us the power and guidance we need to live successful Christian lives. As we all find out, the Christian life isn't hard, it's impossible! That is, it's impossible to live in our own power. Successful Christians learn to lean on His Spirit to empower them to live the Christian life.

Repent and be baptized, every one of you, in the name of Jesus Christ for the forgiveness of your sins. And you will receive the gift of the Holy Spirit. (Acts 2:38)

FUTURE PROMISES

Years ago, I read an interview with an incredible football player. He was a record-setting, professional superstar—the type hero that fans are tempted to worship. But while this quick and powerful running back was confident on the playing field, he wasn't so confident about a bigger issue. One day, an interviewer asked him what he feared—an interesting question for a player so intimidating that his opponents feared him. But his answer was revealing. What did he fear? In his own words, *"Dying and going to hell. But I hope I don't, because I've been a good person."*

This man had risen to the top of his profession, but couldn't find abiding peace because he didn't know for certain where he was headed for eternity. Many people don't even think it's possible to know their eternal destiny. Yet, the Scriptures make it clear:

I write these things to you who believe in the name of the Son of God so that you may know that you have eternal life. (I John 5:13)

To know, not to merely hope or think probable, God wants us to have a confidence and peace about our final destiny. We should be looking forward to spending eternity with Him in our heavenly home!

God promises in His Word that we will:

Escape God's wrath. Since God is a just God, the penalty for sin must be paid. Yet, because of God's grace, Jesus took God's entire wrath for sin upon Himself.

Since we have now been justified by His blood, how much more shall we be saved from God's wrath through Him! (Romans 5:9)

Be resurrected at Christ's second coming. Both deceased believers and the ones alive at His coming will be transformed, receiving new, glorified bodies. The more aches and pains my earthly body gets, the more I get excited about my new heavenly model!

So will it be with the resurrection of the dead. The body that is sown is perishable, it is raised imperishable; it is sown in dishonor, it is raised in glory; it is sown in weakness, it is raised in power; it is sown a natural body, it is raised a spiritual body. (I Corinthians 15:42-44)

Have eternal life. All believers are promised to be with Jesus forever! We don't have to wait to see if we get eternal life. We possess it now!

For God so loved the world that He gave His one and only Son, that whoever believes in Him shall not perish but have eternal life. (John 3:16)

DEALING WITH DOUBTS

If God promised that we will escape His wrath, receive a new heavenly body and live with Him forever, then why do some Christians struggle with doubts? Even if you don't personally struggle with doubt, you will run across others who do. Let's deal with some common causes of doubt.

In the previous Pocket Principle™ we answered two sources of doubt. 1)"I'm not sure that I understood everything when I first accepted Christ." 2)"Sometimes I don't feel saved." Do you remember how we dealt with these? Here are some more.

1. "It's hard to believe God could forgive my past."

Listen to the testimony of this great sinner:

…I was once a blasphemer and a persecutor and a violent man…. Here is a trustworthy saying that deserves full acceptance: Christ Jesus came into the world to save sinners — of whom I am the worst. But for that very reason I was shown mercy so that in me, the worst of sinners, Christ Jesus might display his unlimited patience as an example for those who would believe on him and receive eternal life.

Do you know who wrote that? It was the Apostle Paul in I Timothy 1:13-16, the man who God used to write most of the books of the New Testament. Do you know what he was like before he became a Christian? He rejected Jesus as the Messiah. He was such a violent man and so furiously enraged at Christians that he persecuted the church, imprisoning Christians and having them beaten and killed (I Timothy 1:13; Acts 7:58, 8:1, 9:1,2,4,5, 22:4,5,7,19,20, 26:9-11). But Paul wants you to know that if God can still have mercy on him, then nobody is too bad for God to save. No matter what you've done, remember—

...the blood of Jesus, His Son, purifies us from all sin. (I John 1:7)

From how much sin? "All sin." Even if you've abused drugs or committed sexual sins? "All sin." Even if you've killed Christians? "All sin."

> There's no sin in your past that's so bad that God can't take out the stain and leave you as clean as fresh snow.

2. "To be perfectly honest, I'm not very serious about this God stuff."

Although Harry prayed to receive Jesus at a high school retreat and presently goes to church a couple of times a month, he really doesn't give much thought to God in his day to day living. He doesn't read his Bible to find out how to run his business, raise his children or treat his wife. In fact, his life is really no different from the non-Christians he works with every day. Although he has doubts about his salvation, he's banking on that high school decision at a retreat to get him into heaven.

Harry needs to read some verses that comfort the disturbed, but disturb the comforted. Harry needs to be disturbed. Do you remember the verse we mentioned earlier in this study?

I write these things to you who believe in the name of the Son of God so that you may know that you have eternal life. (I John 5:13)

What were "these things" that John had written to give them assurance? The book of I John describes two kinds of lives, the life of those who have eternal life and the life of those who don't. Look at the characteristics of each life:

Real Christians show evidence of their salvation by their…

Obedience (I John 2:3,4)

We know that we have come to know Him if we obey His commands. The man who says, "I know Him," but does not do what He commands is a liar, and the truth is not in him.

Faith (I John 5:1)

Everyone who believes that Jesus is the Christ is born of God, and everyone who loves the Father loves His child as well.

Love

Love for God (I John 5:1,2)

Everyone who believes that Jesus is the Christ is born of God, and everyone who loves the Father loves His child as well. This is how we know that we love the children of God: by loving God and carrying out His commands.

Love for People (I John 3:14,15)

We know that we have passed from death to life, because we love each other. Anyone who does not love remains in death. Anyone who hates a brother or sister is a murderer, and you know that no murderer has eternal life residing in him.

Although our lifestyle gives evidence of our salvation, it isn't what causes or keeps our salvation.

Some of us sensitive types may look at this list and get discouraged. After all, none of us live out faith, love and obedience 100% of the time. Does this mean we're not Christians? No! When John wrote the book of I John, he often used a tense that in the original Greek indicates a habitual lifestyle. I John 1:8 clarifies that we're not speaking of perfection.

If we claim to be without sin, we deceive ourselves and the truth is not in us.

Some people get so sensitive that when they miss a personal time with God they question whether they are saved or not. But just the fact that you are trying to meet with God, and feel bad when you don't, shows that the Spirit is working in your life.

When we accepted Christ, a big about face occurred in our lives. Instead of making all decisions centered on "me, me, me," we're starting to think about loving others and living for God.

According to I John, my assurance is based, not on how emotional I got at a religious service, but on the general direction of my heart and life, here and now.

Do you believe in Jesus now? Are you following Jesus now? Do you love your brothers and sisters in Christ now? Are you following God rather than following self? According to God's Word you're a Christian and you have eternal life.

Caution! Although our lifestyle gives evidence of our salvation, it isn't what causes or keeps our salvation. Our salvation is by grace through faith, not something we earn (Ephesians 2:8,9).

3. "I'm afraid I'm too weak to hold onto my salvation."

I've got good news for you! First, you don't have to wait to see if you get eternal life with God after you die. You already have eternal life.

> *Our salvation is dependent, not on our ability to hold onto it, but on God's commitment and ability to keep us.*

I write these things to you who believe in the name of the Son of God so that you may know that you have eternal life. (I John 5:13)

Think about it. If you could lose your eternal life, then it was never eternal in the first place! You already possess the eternal life that you're afraid you might not get!

Second, God promises that He'll keep you. Our salvation is dependent, not on our ability to hold onto it, but on God's commitment and ability to keep us. Jesus said,

And this is the will of Him who sent me, that I shall lose none of all that He has given me, but raise them up at the last day. For my Father's will is that everyone who looks to the Son and believes in Him shall have eternal life, and I will raise them up at the last day. (John 6:39, 40)

My sheep listen to my voice; I know them, and they follow me. I give them eternal life, and they shall never perish; no one can snatch them out of my hand. My Father, who has given them to me, is greater than all; no one can snatch them out of my Father's hand. (John 10:27-29)

These verses paint a vivid picture of us securely held in Jesus' and God's hands. Don't let that picture leave your mind. We're not dangling from God's fingers, holding on desperately for fear that we'll fall away from Him. His all-powerful hand holds us so firmly in its grasp that nothing can snatch us away. Our salvation is as secure as the power of God to hold and keep us!

End Notes:

(1) Found in Bill Bright's *Transferable Concepts* (Campus Crusade for Christ). Worded by Steve Miller.

(2) Corrie ten Boom with Jamie Buckingham, *Tramp for the Lord* (Fort Washington, PA: CLC Publications, 1974), 53.

How Can I Be Sure? **Part II**
Prescription For Doubters

Important to Leader: Answers and notes to leaders are in gray, italicized text.

GOAL:

For the disciple to realize what some of the benefits of being a Christian are and to be certain of her salvation.

GETTING STARTED:

What are some of the things people worry about or have doubts about?

Job security, having enough money to pay bills, getting old (health declining), local sports team losing, how our children will turn out, if our life will mean something, etc.

What are some doubts you (or someone you know) have about your salvation?

Transition: *God wants us to be sure about our salvation and has provided pertinent information in His Word.*

STUDYING TOGETHER:

In the Bible, God promises us incredible benefits, both now and in the future.

Read Romans 4:7; II Corinthians 5:17; Acts 2:38.

1. What *present* benefit does each verse promise? What is the significance of each promise to the Christian?

    Romans 4:7: Present Benefit:

    Forgiveness—This removes sin as the barrier between God and us.

    Significance:

    We can have confidence that we are able to come to God and communicate with Him.

    II Corinthians 5:17: Present Benefit:

    New creation—The Christian is a new person, who has a new relationship with God that changes everything (desires, perspective on life, access to God, etc.)

Significance:

This really is a new life! We still have our personalities, differences, etc., but our desires and motivations are new.

Acts 2:38: Present Benefit:

Holy Spirit—God gives the gift of the Holy Spirit to every new believer. (Leader: Be sure that students recognize that the Holy Spirit is God. The Holy Spirit is the topic of a future session in this series.)

Significance:

The Holy Spirit gives us the power to live the way God wants us to.

Read Matthew 25:31-34,41; I Corinthians 15:42-44; John 3:16.

2. What *future* benefits do these verses promise? What is the significance of each promise to Christians?

    Matthew 25:31-34, 41: Future Benefit:

    Believers will receive a Kingdom instead of God's wrath.

    Significance:

    We will receive a reward instead of condemnation.

    I Corinthians 15:42-44: Future Benefit:

    Believers will be resurrected and receive a new (glorified) body at the second coming of Christ.

    Significance:

    Death isn't the end for a Christian, and we will get a new body.

    John 3:16: Future Benefit:

    Believers have eternal life.

    Significance:

    We will spend eternity with God.

Read John 6:37-40.

3. According to these verses, what gives the believer assurance that she has salvation?

God is able to keep all believers, not one will be lost. God has promised to resurrect believers on the last day.

Read John 10:27-30.

4. These verses are similar to the John 6 passage, but add some additional thoughts. What are the additional thoughts?

Jesus' sheep listen to His voice and follow Him. No one can take a believer out of Jesus' hand and the Father's hand.

So far, we have seen that we can have assurance of salvation because of God's ability to keep us in His family once we are Christians. But, how can we be assured we are Christians in the first place?

Read I John 2:3; I John 5:1a; I John 4:7.

5. In these verses, John gives evidence that a person is a Christian. What is the evidence given in each verse?

Obedience, faith, and love for others and for God.

After reading these verses, we may conclude we are doomed for sure! After all, none of us live out obedience, faith and love 100% of the time. Does that mean we're not Christians? NO!!!!

We don't instantly become perfect. We grow as Christians. It's a process. As a Christian you should be growing in your desire to exhibit these traits, and in your ability to express them. Desire and growth give evidence of God's presence in your life.

Read I John 1:8,10.

According to these verses, God knows we're not perfect and assures us we can KNOW we have eternal life. Additionally, if we are seeking to obey Jesus in our words and actions, believing in Him as our Savior and Lord, and seeking to love Him and His people, we are demonstrating evidence of the Christian life.

LOOKING AT REAL LIFE:

6. Why do you think it is important to have evidence that we are Christians?

    Having these evidences helps us assure others and ourselves that we have entered into a relationship with God. When threatened with doubt, we are able to look back at the evidences and assure ourselves that we are believers.

7. If a person is confident that he is a believer, what difference will this make in the way he lives his life?

    It will be easier to be bold about his testimony and sharing his faith. It will be easier to trust God and exercise faith. He will be more open to growing spiritually. He will be more confident when he encounters difficulties.

8. Look back over some of the benefits of becoming a Christian. (See questions #1 and #2.) If a believer keeps these benefits in mind, how will it change her life?

    She will have confidence in her relationship with God. Her desires and motives will change to be in line with God's. She realizes she has power available beyond herself. She knows that how she lives here on earth counts for eternity. She knows there is a better life coming.

LOOKING AT MY LIFE:

What are the evidences you see in your life that you have a relationship with God?

Explain your answer.

Were any of your doubts (or those of your friends) addressed by this lesson? If so, explain. (Not every doubt can be addressed in one study, so your concern may not have been mentioned. Please share any other troubling doubts with your leader.)

Baptism
Going Public

Imagine that Dave and Rhonda met at a fraternity party at the University of Georgia. Mutual friends had been telling them they should meet, since they had so much in common—a love for sports, highly competitive, and both preparing to teach middle school. Their first glimpse of each other was through a volleyball net in a "friendly" game in the front yard of the frat house. It was anything but love at first sight. Towards the end of the game, with the score tied and adrenaline pumping through their veins, both jumped up for a ball and Rhonda spiked it into Dave's face, thoroughly humiliating him. On the next point, he returned the favor with a blistering serve that almost sprained her wrists. Their friends had to break up the fight!

But later that evening, trading stories of high school sports and their shared passion to make middle school more tolerable for students, they had to admit that they had a lot in common. Within months, they had fallen in love. During their senior year, after a meal at a romantic restaurant, Dave popped the question: "Rhonda, I don't want to see anyone else but you. Will you be my wife?" Rhonda had been half-expecting the proposal, but was still overcome with emotion.

"Of course!" was all she could say. "When should we have the wedding?" After an awkward silence, Dave said, "You know that I've never been a very traditional person. Why should we spend the time and money for a formal ceremony, when we already know that we're committed in our hearts for life? Besides, you know that I'm scared to death to say anything in front of a group of people. I don't know if I could handle all those vows and the 'I do's.'"

If you were Rhonda, how would you answer Dave?

> **If we are serious about Christ, we need to go public with our decision.**

A wedding is a public announcement of a private decision. It tells the world, "We're taking ourselves out of the dating pool. We're taking the plunge. We're committing our lives to each other."

Similar to Dave and Rhonda's relationship, you may have started your relationship with God on bad terms. Perhaps you resented someone wanting to intrude on your life. But eventually, after some mutual friends helped you to understand His love and trustworthiness, you realized that you were more than ready to trade in your old master (yourself and sin) for a more worthy Master. As a member of a 12-step group said, "When I turned my life over to God, I took my life out of the hands of an idiot!"

Yet, contrary to much popular opinion, a relationship with God isn't just a private matter. If we're serious about Him, we need to go public with our decision. New Testament believers went public through baptism. In this session, we'll study both the importance and meaning of baptism.

WHY GET BAPTIZED?

As Christians, we're followers of Christ. Since Jesus was baptized (Luke 3:21), shouldn't we follow His example? If we think we should follow Him in His example of love for people and commitment to the Father, why not follow Him in His example of baptism?

Someone might object, "What if baptism is just one of those cultural things Jesus did, like wearing sandals and walking everywhere He went?" To make sure we didn't get confused on this point, He baptized His followers and commanded that future followers be baptized.

After this, Jesus and his disciples went out into the Judean countryside, where He spent some time with them, and baptized. (John 3:22)

Therefore go and make disciples of all nations, baptizing them…. (Matthew 28:19)

> The idea of cleansing is used in New Testament times as a picture of Christian baptism.

The book of Acts, our inspired record of the early church, gives the impression that an unbaptized believer was unheard of.

Those who accepted his message were baptized…. (Acts 2:41, cross reference 8:12)

You may ask, "But do some churches dunk and some sprinkle? Which is right?" Throughout church history, different traditions have been followed concerning the mode of baptism. Talk to your church leaders about why they baptize in the way that they do. Our goal in this study is simply to understand the meaning and importance of baptism.

WHAT BAPTISM PICTURES

Like a wedding ring, baptism is symbolic. The Bible gives us three pictures of what baptism means.

Picture #1. Cleansing From Sin. During Old Testament times, if a Jew became defiled by touching something that God had declared unclean (like a corpse), God's law instructed him to be sprinkled with water that was connected with a sacrificed animal. This purified him from his uncleanness. (See, for example, Numbers 19.) Since Jesus sacrificed Himself for our sins, He fulfilled all the ceremonial law for us so that we no longer have to follow all those rules and regulations to be purified.

Yet, the idea of cleansing is used in New Testament times as a picture of Christian baptism. I John 1:9 says,

If we confess our sins, He is faithful and righteous to forgive us our sins and to cleanse us from all unrighteousness. (NASB)

"Cleanse" pictures washing away the "dirtiness" and "stains" of our sins, resulting in our forgiveness. But what happens when we continue to sin after our "purification" at salvation? John tells us,

But if we walk in the light, as He is in the light, we have fellowship with one another, and the blood of Jesus, His Son, purifies us from all sin. (I John 1:7)

In other words, since none of us can live perfect lives, God continues to cleanse us from sin through Jesus' blood. We keep in fellowship with Him on a day-by-day and minute-by-minute basis by confessing (agreeing with God or admitting) our sins to Him. When you disobey God, simply confess to Him that you blew it. You don't have to try to make it up to God or torture yourself. Jesus took all that punishment upon Himself so that we wouldn't have to! Just confess it to God, receive His forgiveness, ask Him for the power to keep living for Him, and keep going.

Picture #2. Identification With Christ. A second picture of baptism is union with Christ, becoming one with Him. During the time of Christ, the word "baptism" was used to describe the process of dyeing fabric. Someone would dip ("baptize") the fabric in the dye, allowing the fabric to absorb the dye. After the dipping, it was no longer possible to separate the fabric from the dye. They were "one."

In the same way, when a Christian is baptized, it's like being dipped into Christ and becoming united or one with Him. Because we are one with Christ, many things that are true of Christ become true of us. For example, we share in His death and resurrection. (See Romans 6:3-11.)

For all of you who were baptized into Christ have been clothed with Christ. (Galatians 3:27)

Picture #3. Identification With the Church. Enthusiastic fans of a college team will find some way to let others know. A true Georgia Tech fan will place his team's bumper sticker on his car, identifying himself with his team. He is in no way embarrassed to be identified publicly with his team. Some fans show up at games with their bodies painted in the team colors!

In the book of Acts we find people publicly identifying themselves with Christ and His Church through baptism.

Those who accepted his message were baptized…. (Acts 2:41)

In some cultures that are hostile to Christianity, the people can often tolerate those who merely attend a Christian church, but when they get baptized, everyone knows that they've broken ties with their old religion to identify themselves with Christianity. Many are persecuted or even killed because of their baptism.

> There's no sin in your past that's so bad that God can't take out the stain and leave you as clean as fresh snow.

In some churches baptism is associated with joining a particular local church and serves to initiate a person into that church. In other churches, people are baptized who accept Christ whether or not they want to join that local church.

Some churches baptize infants, viewing baptism as an initiation into a community of believers committed to raise the child to know and follow Jesus. Most churches don't see this as guaranteeing salvation. Each person must make his or her own decision to receive Jesus.

SHARING YOUR DECISION WITH FRIENDS AND FAMILY

Baptism is a public announcement of a private decision. Some may want to know more about how you made this decision, others may voice concerns, and some may even resist the idea of you trading your old life of serving self for a new life of following Christ. So the question arises, "What should you tell others about becoming a Christian?"

Since everyone is unique, we must all tell our own story of how we came to faith in Christ. But the following guidelines may help you frame your conversations in ways that will help others better understand.

Tell your story. When questions come up, tell others what made you aware that you needed Christ. Share the feelings, thoughts, and circumstances that convinced you of your need to follow Him. Remember, it's your story. Keep it personal.

Keep it simple. The Gospel is part of your story. It's the good news that you believed to be saved and it's both clear and simple:

> Christ died for sins (and everyone sins).
> He rose from the dead.
> He offers forgiveness and a relationship with Him.

As you learn more about the Gospel, you'll be able to explain its message in more detail.

Avoid arguments. The Good News is that Christ died for everyone. But not everyone may be ready to make that decision. Some may have sincere questions about your new faith. Others may be uncomfortable with your decision for various reasons. It may put pressure on them to examine themselves. They may be hostile to Christianity or believe spiritual matters are private. Answer questions as best as you can, but avoid arguments. As you grow, your changed life will provide evidence that something is different about you.

CONCLUSION

If you are a believer in Christ but haven't been baptized, make plans to participate in this meaningful event. If you haven't found a church to attend, let your Christian friends recommend one and then talk to the church staff about baptism. Congratulations on identifying yourself with Jesus!

Baptism
Going Public

Important to Leader: Answers and notes to leaders are in gray, italicized text.

Note: In this study there are quite a few comments (i.e. not questions). In these studies we want to let the Bible "speak for itself." However, there are few direct, clear passages about baptism so it is difficult to write discussion questions for new believers.

GOAL:

For the disciple to understand the meaning and significance of baptism.

GETTING STARTED:

Exchanging wedding rings is a common ritual. What does a wedding ring signify?

It is the visible token of the commitment of the couple to each other, a beginning investment in their marriage. The circular shape of the ring is a symbol of never-ending love. It communicates the couple's commitment to each other.

Transition: In a similar way, baptism is a Christian ritual that is rich in meaning. In this study we will gain a better understanding of the meaning of baptism.

STUDYING TOGETHER & LOOKING AT REAL LIFE:

Read Matthew 3:13-17; John 3:22; Matthew 28:18-20.

1. What conclusions about baptism can you draw from these verses?

   Jesus Himself was baptized. He baptized His followers. And He commanded His followers to baptize new believers.

The Bible uses 3 pictures to describe baptism.

First picture: cleansing from sin (forgiveness). (Acts 2:38)

There were various forms of "washings" or "baptisms" for purification found in the Old Testament. God set forth laws in the Old Testament for ceremonial cleansing or purification. In Numbers 19 there is an example of how to be purified through a series of washings if a person had been defiled in some way.

However, the idea of cleansing and purification is brought forward into the New Testament and pictured in Christian baptism. Cleansing is a picture of having the dirtiness and stain of our sins washed away. This cleansing results in our forgiveness.

2. How is having this picture of being "washed clean" helpful to you?

The image of washing helps me understand that I'm clean before God and helps me feel clean. Think of taking a shower, the refreshing way you feel afterwards.

Read I John 1:9.

3. Why do we need to confess our sins daily if Christ died for all of our sins?

Christ died for all our sins, and they are all forgiven. However when we sin, it disrupts our relationship with God and that needs to be restored by our confession of the sin. (Think about the relationships in a family. If you have conflict with each other or sin against each other, your relationship is strained until there is confession and forgiveness given. But regardless, you are still family!)

Second picture: Identification with Christ (a picture of union with Christ or becoming one with Christ).

In the time of Christ, the word "baptism" was used to describe the process of dyeing fabric. One would dip ("baptize") the fabric in the dye and the fabric would absorb the dye. Then, it would no longer be possible to separate the fabric from the dye. They would be "one."

Read Galatians 3:27.

4. What does "being clothed in Christ" mean?

I am so closely identified with Christ that when God looks at me, He sees Christ.

When a Christian is baptized, he is, so to speak, dipped into Christ and thus becomes united or one with Christ. He is one with Christ to such a degree that, in some senses, what is true of Christ becomes true of him from God's perspective.

In some Christian denominations baptism is associated with joining a particular local church and acts as an initiation into that church.

In some churches, which practice infant baptism, baptism is seen as an initiation into a community of believers where the child can be raised in the nurture and admonition of the Lord. This does not guarantee salvation. Each person must make his own decision at some point in his life.

5. If we fully understand our identity with Christ, how should that affect how we look at ourselves as Christians?

We should see ourselves as God sees us (as like Christ) in spite of the fact that we still struggle with sin. We shouldn't be judgmental of ourselves. We should have hope that our life will change.

Third picture: Identification with the Church

Read Acts 2:38-41.

6. What things do we learn about the practice of baptism in the early church from these verses?

Sometimes new believers were baptized immediately (if possible) after they made a commitment. People were told they should be baptized. Baptism was a public act.

Read Acts 2:42.

7. What did those who were baptized do afterwards, according to these verses?

They began to meet with other believers (the church) on a regular basis. Some of the things they did: listened to the teaching of the leaders, prayed, fellowshipped with each other. In summary, they became an active part of the church.

8. How does being baptized in public help a new believer?

Challenges the new believer to proclaim her decision for Christ publicly, confirms her step of faith to herself and to others, informs the local church that they have a new family member.If the new believer has doubts in the future about her relationship with Christ, she can look back and be encouraged about her commitment.

9. Why do you think God gave us these pictures of baptism?

LOOKING AT MY LIFE:

If you *have not been baptized,* are there any hindrances to being baptized? If so, what are they? How can these be overcome?

OR

If you *have been baptized,* share your experience with the group.

If you *are a believer and you have not been baptized,* find a good church in the area where you live and talk to the pastor about being baptized. If you have additional questions about baptism, talk with your pastor.

If you have been baptized, please refer to page 23 in the Pocket Principle™ *Baptism* and review the content under the heading "Sharing Your Decision With Friends And Family." Write out your story about becoming a Christian, and read it to the group.

The Holy Spirit
God Comes To Live In Us

BREATHTAKING RESCUES

During the war with Iraq, America's elite Special Forces pulled off two breathtaking rescues of our POWs from behind enemy lines. In the first, Jessica Lynch lay in grave physical condition, with wounds to her head and back and many broken bones. She was way beyond using her skills, wits and training to mastermind an escape. Even if she could crawl to the door, four Iraqi soldiers waited there, armed with AK-47 machine guns. All the strength she could muster was futile. Her only hope was to be rescued.

That's exactly where we found ourselves spiritually before our salvation. We were lost, without hope, without the resources or ability to reach heaven on our own. Fortunately, God came to our rescue. As the Apostle Paul put it,

For He rescued us from the domain of darkness, and transferred us to the kingdom of His beloved Son.... (Colossians 1:13, NASB)

I want someone to accompany me through this life, someone strong enough to take care of me.

Fortunately (or providentially!) for Jessica, an awesome array of Special Forces risked their lives to come for her. After midnight, hundreds of Marines crossed enemy lines and created a diversion south of Jessica's building with artillery and gunfire. Then, several dozen "door-kickers" arrived in Black Hawk helicopters provided by Air Force special operations. Army Rangers secured the building. Navy Seals penetrated the hospital.

Wearing night goggles, the Seals found her room and whisked her off to a helicopter. But, although she was rescued, she knew that she wasn't out of harm's way. On the helicopter, she said, "Please don't let anyone leave me." They never did.

Lest you think this desperation for companionship was just a feminine reaction to her ordeal, in a similar rescue of 7 male POWs in Iraq, the rescuers sensed the same need for companionship in the rescued men. So, two Marines were instructed by their commanding officer to accompany the soldiers out of Iraq. As one rescuer said, "We were the first Americans they'd seen since they were captured. They kind of clung to us from the start, so our Commanding Officer figured they needed some familiar faces traveling with them." [1]

Spiritually, I have some of the same needs and feelings as these POWs. Sure, I've been rescued from darkness and given a new chance at life. But I don't want to be simply dumped outside the city limits of Baghdad and left to fend for myself. I want someone to accompany me through this life, someone strong enough to take care of me.

This is exactly what God has given us in His Holy Spirit. When Jesus readied His disciples for His departure, He assured them that He'd send them a "helper"—"one summoned to the side of another to befriend him, advise him, and if necessary plead his cause."[2] (John 14:16,26, 15:26, 16:7)

But the Helper, the Holy Spirit, whom the Father will send in My name, He will teach you all things, and bring to your remembrance all that I said to you. (John 14:26, NASB)

And, He comes to live inside of us! In this Pocket Principle™, we'll learn more about the Holy Spirit and how He wants to relate to us.

WHEN GOD MOVED IN

Back in Old Testament times, God wasn't as up close and personal. Sure, He talked to Moses face to face, but to most of God's people, He was separated from them by a veil in the temple. God dwelt "in the midst of" His people (Exodus 15:13,17; Numbers 35:34; Deuteronomy 7:21). The temple symbolized God's presence (Deuteronomy 12:5-7), and only the priests could enter the "holy of holies," where God could be contacted.

You shall not dread them, for the LORD your God is in your midst, a great and awesome God. (Deuteronomy 7:21, NASB)

God moved out of His temple and into His people!

Jesus changed all of that. In the Christmas story, you may remember Jesus is referred to as "Immanuel," which means "God is with us." (Matthew 1:23) God walked among us during His years on earth, but He assured His disciples that after His death and resurrection He'd stay close to them through His indwelling Spirit (John 14:7). When He died on the cross, the temple veil ripped in two, symbolizing that God's presence was no longer just for the priests (Matthew 27:51).

When He ascended, He told His disciples to go to Jerusalem and wait for the Holy Spirit. Since that time, the Holy Spirit enters believers at the time of our salvation (Acts 2:38; Ephesians 1:13; Romans 8:9-11). Now all believers are priests; our bodies are His temple (I Corinthians 6:19; Acts 17:24). God moved out of His temple and into His people!

Do you not know that your body is a temple of the Holy Spirit, who is in you, whom you have received from God? (I Corinthians 6:19)

When a young child named Benji expressed a strong desire to make sure that he was going to heaven, his parents led him in a prayer to ask Jesus to come live in his heart. After the prayer, Benji looked up at his parents with a confident smile and said, "Well, He's packing!" In his literal-thinking mind, Benji could imagine God packing His bags to come live in his heart. What a great picture!

When God's Spirit comes to live in us, He makes several changes in our lives.

A NEW LIFE

One night, Jesus talked to a fellow named Nicodemus about how to enter God's kingdom. Being a high ranking Pharisee, Nicodemus had certainly studied God's Word and tried to live it out. Yet, Jesus said that he couldn't get into God's kingdom without being born again, which He also calls being born of the Spirit (John 3:5). Jesus was speaking of the new life the Spirit gives to us.

Jesus also described this new life as crossing from death to life (John 5:24). Those who have not been born again are spiritually dead. Only when the Spirit of God enters their lives do they become spiritually alive (Ephesians 2:1-5). This means not only that the believer has eternal life, but that additionally he has a personal relationship with God (is alive to Him).

> Although this new relationship with God, through the Holy Spirit, begins at salvation, it keeps growing throughout the rest of our lives.

Although this new relationship with God, through the Holy Spirit, begins at salvation, it keeps growing throughout the rest of our lives. It's kind of like a good marriage. A couple becomes one on their wedding day, but they continue to grow in their relationship throughout their lives. Two of the Holy Spirit's continuing ministries are to assure the believer that she is a child of God and to inspire her to cry out to God, her Father, in prayer (Romans 8:15-16).

For you did not receive a spirit that makes you a slave again to fear, but you received the Spirit of sonship. And by Him we cry, 'Abba, Father.' The Spirit himself testifies with our spirit that we are God's children. (Romans 8:15,16)

A NEW HEART

Cassie Bernall became known worldwide as a 17-year-old student who died in the April, 1999 massacre at Columbine High School. Although she was a committed Christian at the time of her death, she wasn't always that way. Raised by loving parents, she got with the wrong friends and began to dabble in satanic rituals. Subtly, the glasses through which she viewed the world became darker and darker, until she could seem to find no good in the world. She would cut herself. She hated her parents, God and her life, becoming obsessed with suicide. Cassie wouldn't have responded to a self-help book or a motivational speech. She needed a new heart.

Her mom began to pray desperately. A Christian classmate befriended her and wouldn't let go. She invited Cassie to a weekend retreat in the Rocky Mountains. During a praise and worship service, God broke through. Her change was immediate and dramatic. She walked outside the meeting room with some friends, gazed at the stars and stood in awe of the God she once hated.

When her parents met her at the bus, they immediately saw the difference. According to her dad, "it was as if she had been in a dark room, and somebody had turned the light on, and she could suddenly see the beauty surrounding her." They saw the smile that had disappeared years ago. God had given her a new heart—one that had a passion to love God and love people. [3] Before we knew Christ, we had serious heart problems. We needed more than corrective surgery; we needed a transplant.

What does it mean to have a new heart? An Old Testament Prophet named Ezekiel prophesied of a time when God would send His Spirit to live within believers and give them new hearts. He said that God would remove their hearts of stone and give them hearts of flesh (Ezekiel 36:26). A "heart of flesh" means a heart that is responsive to God. It seeks after Him and desires to follow Him (Ezekiel 36:27).

I will give you a new heart and put a new spirit in you; I will remove from you your heart of stone and give you a heart of flesh. And I will put my Spirit in you and move you to follow my decrees and be careful to keep my laws. (Ezekiel 36:26, 27)

The Apostle Paul explained the same truth in a different way. He spoke of the "desires of the Spirit." (Galatians 5:17; Romans 8:5) When we are born again, the Holy Spirit gives us a new set of godly desires. But many sinful desires remain as well. God's indwelling Spirit gives us the power to say "yes" to the godly desires and "no" to the sinful ones (Galatians 5:16,22-23).

A NEW PERSPECTIVE

The Holy Spirit enlightens our understanding (I Corinthians 2:12). Those who do not have the Spirit (unbelievers) do not understand the things of God. Spiritual issues seem like foolishness to them (I Corinthians 2:14). We see this dramatic change in the Apostle Paul. Before his conversion, he saw Christianity as a perversion of the truth. After receiving the Holy Spirit, he understood the truth (Acts 9:17-18).

We have not received the spirit of the world but the Spirit who is from God, that we may understand what God has freely given us. (I Corinthians 2:12)

Of course, the Spirit doesn't give us all spiritual knowledge. We won't see all things clearly until we're in heaven (I Corinthians 13:12). Here on earth the Spirit opens our eyes immediately to some truths, and others as we follow Him and read His Word. It's kind of like taking a trip by car at night. When you turn on the headlights, you can't see all the way to your destination, but as you move forward, your headlights give enough light to let you continue your journey.

CONCLUSION

We introduced this lesson by describing the dramatic rescue of Jessica Lynch. It wasn't enough to be rescued. She needed someone to accompany and protect her until she could make it home. As I write, she's safely home in America, celebrating her 20th birthday. God not only rescued us from the domain of darkness, but also promised to accompany us each step of our journey—helping us, enlightening us, growing us up, and transforming us until that day that we arrive safely at our heavenly home.

End Notes:

(1) Sgt. Joseph R. Chenelly, Marines Recount POW Rescue Operation, I Marine Expeditionary Force. Patrick Rogers, Peter Mikelbank, Rose Ellen O'Connor, Susan Keating, Jane Sims Podesta, Courtney Rubin, "Saved From Danger," *People*, (April 21, 2003).

(2) R.V.G. Tasker, *Book of John, Tyndale New Testament Commentaries* (Grand Rapids, MI: Wm. B. Eerdmans Publishing Company, 1960), 172.

(3) Misty Bernall, *She Said Yes: The Unlikely Martyrdom of Cassie Bernall* (Rifton, NY: Plough Publishers, 1999).

The Holy Spirit

God Comes To Live In Us

Important to Leader: Answers and notes to leaders are in gray, italicized text.

GOAL:

For the disciple to understand the indwelling of the Holy Spirit and how the Spirit changes the life of the new believer.

GETTING STARTED:

If you won $10 million in the lottery, how would your life change?

Need to get an investment advisor. Relatives and friends may initiate the idea that you should give them some (since you have so much). You would become a focus of the media and be asked lots of questions (What are you going to do...?). Money would become a greater focus in your life. Decisions would need to be made about what to do with the money. You would stop worrying about retirement and paying bills.

Transition: God has given us even a greater gift, the Holy Spirit, which changes our life in profound ways.

STUDYING TOGETHER:

Read Exodus 40:34-38.

1. According to these verses in the Old Testament, when God was forming the nation of Israel, where did He reside in relationship to His people?

   He dwelt in the tabernacle, which was a special tent that God directed them to set up.

2. How did the Israelites know that God was there?

   They could see Him in the fire and in a cloud. (The tabernacle was always in the middle of the Israelites so that everyone could see Him, whether they were camped or were moving.)

Read John 14:16-17; Acts 2:38.

3. According to the New Testament, where does God dwell in relationship to His people?

   When Jesus left His disciples on earth He sent the Holy Spirit to be in them. Later, in Acts, He sent the Holy Spirit to be in all believers.

Read John 3:3-7; John 5:24; Ephesians 2:1,4-5.

4. How do these verses describe what happened to a believer at the moment of salvation?

   He was given a new life in Christ, he is born of the Spirit and he has passed from death to life.

5. What do these descriptions mean?

   A believer's life is changed. We were dead because of our sins, but God, because of His grace, made us alive. The result is that we are alive to God.

Read Ezekiel 36:26-27.

6. Ezekiel was prophesying about a future time when the Holy Spirit would be within them. What did he prophesy?

   That God would give believers a new heart by putting a new spirit within them. The Holy Spirit would replace their heart of stone with a heart of flesh. This will give them a desire to follow God's law.

7. What is the difference between a heart of stone and a heart of flesh?

   The heart of flesh is moldable, responsive to God, while a heart of stone is hard and unresponsive.

Read Galatians 5:17.

8. In this verse, Paul is speaking about the difference the Holy Spirit makes. What is the internal conflict Paul talks about here?

   There is a conflict between the desires of the sin nature and the desires of the Spirit.

   What is the result of this conflict?

   This conflict makes it difficult for a believer to follow God.

Read Galatians 5:16.

9. What does Paul tell believers to do to overcome this conflict?

    Live by the Spirit and don't satisfy the desires of the sinful nature.

    What do you think it means to live by the Spirit?

    To live in dependence on the Spirit, to pray with humility; to ask God to show you His will and give you strength to obey.

Read I Corinthians 2:12.

10. What is another way in which the Spirit of God helps us as Christians?

    He allows us to understand the things of God.

11. What are some ways you can think of that the Spirit helps us understand the things of God?

    Helps us understand the Bible, gives us wisdom in life situations, convicts us of sin, tells us what is true, etc.

LOOKING AT REAL LIFE:

12. Because of the indwelling Holy Spirit, what **should** be the differences between the lives of Christians and non-Christians?

    Christians should desire to follow God and desire to spend time with God, should be excited about the changes in their lives, have a concern about the spiritual life of others, etc.

13. What are some of the benefits to a believer of having a new life in Christ?

    Life will please God, have a sense of peace and purpose, will be able to love others, there is more meaning to life, eternal, etc.

LOOKING AT MY LIFE:

How have you seen the Holy Spirit work in your life? Give evidence of a new life, new heart and new perspective.

Have you felt the conflict between the sin nature and the desires of the Spirit since you've been a Christian? If so, please explain. What can you do about this conflict?

What are some areas in your life you would like to see the Spirit work in and change?

The Bible
The Word Of God

ON MODEL AIRPLANES AND INSTRUCTIONS

Have you ever built a complex model? I'm not talking about the snap-together ones you find in cereal boxes. I'm talking about the models with hundreds of tiny parts, where you use so much glue that you feel intoxicated by the end of the day. Imagine that someone had the audacity to think that he could build a complex model airplane without ever referring to the instructions. Since many of the parts look familiar, he wastes no time gluing the fuselage together, and the cockpit to the fuselage.

But soon, he begins to experience major frustrations. He didn't realize that some of those remaining little parts were to go on the control panel, which is now permanently sealed beneath the windshield. And that tail fin was designed to fit in before the fuselage was glued together. As you can imagine, the final result would be a disaster.

How much more complex is running a business or a family? Fortunately, God didn't leave us to figure out life on our own. He gave us an instruction manual for successful living. As God said to Joshua when he took over the leadership of Israel,

Do not let this Book of the Law depart from your mouth; meditate on it day and night, so that you may be careful to do everything written in it. Then you will be prosperous and successful. (Joshua 1:8)

If we want to live successful lives, we dare not neglect God's instruction book.

MOST AMAZING BOOK EVER WRITTEN!

Anyone searching for spiritual truth would want to consult the Bible. Why? Just think about its:

- Distribution: It's the bestselling book of all time, with no close competitor.

- Translation: It's been read by more people and published in more languages than any other book.

- Accuracy: Over and over, archeologists and historians have proven its historical reliability. According to a renowned Jewish archaeologist, *"It may be stated categorically that no archaeological discovery has ever controverted a biblical reference."* [1]

- Transforming Power: Those who study it and believe it testify that it's the most valuable book ever written. It's the only place a person can go to find God's perspective and direction. It tells us how to have a relationship with God and how to grow in that relationship.

The Bible is certainly a remarkable book! We can even better appreciate its importance by answering several questions about it.

WHO WROTE THE BIBLE?

First, it has dual authorship. The Holy Spirit is one of the authors. But rather than dictate the words in a mechanical way, He revealed truth to human authors and inspired them to write it down in their own words and styles.

All Scripture is God breathed and is useful for teaching, rebuking, correcting and training in righteousness, so that the man of God may be thoroughly equipped for every good work. (II Timothy 3:16)

Above all, you must understand that no prophecy of Scripture came about by the prophet's own interpretation. For prophecy never had its origin in the will of man, but men spoke from God as they were carried along by the Holy Spirit. (II Peter 1:20)

If we want to live successful lives, we dare not neglect God's instruction book.

Since God inspired the Bible, we can be assured that He preserved the human authors from error. We don't have to pick and choose what to believe out of the Bible. Since we follow Jesus as Lord, it makes sense to view the entire Bible as He viewed it. Jesus said,

Do not think that I have come to abolish the Law or the Prophets; I have not come to abolish them but to fulfill them. I tell you the truth, until heaven and earth disappear, not the smallest letter, not the least stroke of a pen, will by any means disappear from the Law until everything is accomplished. (Matthew 5:17-18)

WHY WAS THE BIBLE WRITTEN?

The Bible tells us all about how God dealt with His people through the years. But why did God tell us all this? To satisfy our curiosity? No! He wanted to show us why we're here, who He is, how to connect with Him and how to live.

Your Word is a lamp to my feet and a light for my path. (Psalm 119:105)

Without a word from God, we could not know any of this. Some people think they can find the answers to life through experimentation with the world. But without a word from God (revelation), science fails to give us the answers to life's most important questions.

Nobel Prize winning physicist Erwin Schrodinger came up with arguably the most important equation in science and founded wave mechanics. Although he loved science, he knew its limits. He once said, "I'm very astonished that the scientific picture of the real world is very deficient. It gives a lot of factual information, puts all our experience in a magnificently consistent order, but it is ghastly silent about all and sundry that is really near to our heart, that really matters to us. It cannot tell us a word about red and blue, bitter and sweet, physical pain and physical delight, knows nothing of beautiful and ugly, good or bad, God and eternity. Science sometimes pretends to answer questions in these domains, but the answers are very often so silly that we are not inclined to take them seriously." [2]

> Without a word from God (revelation), science fails to give us the answers to life's most important questions.

Others think they can find life's answers through philosophy. Yet, Frederick Copleston was one of the greatest authorities on philosophy who ever lived. Along with many other books, he wrote the most comprehensive, most respected history of philosophy in existence. Its massive 17 volumes of microscopic print in paperback have been called "one of the enduring intellectual achievements of the twentieth century." (George Weigel)

After an almost single-minded study of philosophy for almost seven decades, did he think that it offered the answers to life? In his autobiography, published a year before his death, he spoke of how his confidence in philosophy's ability to deliver the goods waned over his years of inquiry. He concluded that even the best mind's limited ability "doubtless shows the need for religious Revelation…." [3]

And what place does that revelation of God have in our lives? According to Copleston, "…God did not reveal this or that truth simply to impart some more or less interesting information. Revelation was granted for salvation, to bring human beings to union with God; and Christ is recorded as saying that He came that human beings might have life—and might have it more abundantly." [4]

So God has revealed Himself and His will to mankind through His Word.

HOW IS IT LAID OUT?

The first part of the Bible is called the Old Testament. It has four parts.

"The Pentateuch" or "The Law" (Genesis–Deuteronomy) begins with a fascinating account of the Creation of the world, the beginnings of the Jewish nation, their miraculous escape under the leadership of Moses from Egyptian captivity and the origin of the Ten Commandments.

The Historical Books (Joshua–Esther) After Moses' death, we find Israel first led by Joshua, then a series of Judges and finally a succession of sometimes good and sometimes bad Kings. After "doing what was right in their own eyes" one time too many, God finally allowed another nation to take them over. This got their attention and as a result, their God of infinite patience and mercy allowed them to return to Israel.

The Poetic or Wisdom Literature (Job–Song of Solomon) writings include the devotional writings of King David (Psalms) and the extremely practical wisdom of Solomon (Proverbs).

The Prophets (Isaiah–Malachi) Although prophets sometimes spoke of the future, they were primarily engaged in receiving relevant messages from God and telling these messages to His people. The first five books are called the "Major Prophets," the last twelve the "Minor Prophets." Don't confuse this use of the terms with "Major League Baseball" and "Minor League Baseball." Regarding the prophets, it has nothing to do with their importance or how good they are. The major prophets merely wrote lengthier books than the minor ones did.

The second part of the Bible is called the **New Testament.** It also has four parts.

The Gospels (Matthew–John) are accounts of Jesus' life by four authors who either lived with Him or researched His life from eyewitness testimonies.

Acts gives us a history of the early church.

The Epistles or Letters (Romans–Jude) explain how to understand and live the Christian life. The first thirteen (Pauline Epistles) were written by the Apostle Paul. The final eight (General Epistles) were written by five different authors.

The Revelation is a very symbolic, prophetic letter about the second coming of Jesus, the end of the world as we know it, and God's establishment of a new heaven and new earth.

IS THE BIBLE IN CHRONOLOGICAL ORDER?

In the Old Testament, The Pentateuch and historical books are in chronological order. The rest of the Old Testament fits within the chronology of those historical books.

In the New Testament, the Gospels each go through Jesus' life. Acts continues the history where the Gospels leave off. The letters are ordered by length, not chronologically. Some fit back into the timeline covered by Acts. Others were written later. Revelation was written last.

The chapter and verse divisions were not in the original writings. They were added much later in order to help the reader find specific information.

HOW IS IT UNIQUE?

One day a representative of Great Books of the Western World came to Josh McDowell's home, trying to recruit him as a salesman. After describing the Great Books series, McDowell challenged him to take "just 10 of the authors, all from one walk of life, one generation, one place, one time, one mood, one continent, one language and just one controversial subject…." Then he asked, "Would they agree?" The recruiter responded "No!" McDowell asked, "What would you have?" He immediately responded, "A conglomeration."

A couple of days later, the recruiter committed his life to Christ.[5] Apparently McDowell had shared the following information about the Bible:

- Consists of 66 books

- Composed by 40 different authors

- Written over a span of 1600 years

- By men from all walks of life, under different conditions, on three different continents, in three languages, concerning hundreds of controversial subjects.

Yet in spite of all these variations, it addresses hundreds of controversial subjects with harmony and unity throughout. Now that's miraculous!

ACTION POINTS

How can we get the most out of the Bible? *First*, pray that the Holy Spirit will both motivate you to study God's Word and help you to understand it. A part of the Spirit's job is to reveal God's truth.

We have not received the spirit of the world but the Spirit who is from God, that we may understand what God has freely given us. This is what we speak, not in words taught us by human wisdom but in words taught by the Spirit, expressing spiritual truths in spiritual words. (I Corinthians 2:12-13)

Second, apply yourself to read, discuss, pray over and obey God's Word.

…like newborn babes, long for the pure milk of the word, so that by it you may grow in respect to salvation, if you have tasted the kindness of the Lord. (I Peter 2:2,3, NASB)

I heard of a primitive tribe who cooks their meat by covering it with sand and building a fire over it. Problem is, some of the sand stays in the meat, with the long-term side effect of grinding down their teeth. So, in order to feed the elderly members, younger members actually chew up the food for them, giving the pre-chewed meat to their grateful elders.

As gross as this may sound, many Christians think nothing of surviving off predigested Bible passages. They rely totally on the teachings of others, rather than using their full set of healthy teeth to feast on the Word, reading and meditating on it for themselves. God wants better for His children. Eat it fresh!

But what if you really hate reading or the Bible seems as dry as dust to you? Here's what one young man did. He knew from the above passage that it was God's will for him to crave God's Word. He also knew from I John 5:14,15 that God promises to give us whatever we ask for that's in His will.

Follow God's instruction book and you'll avoid many of life's disasters.

This is the confidence we have in approaching God: that if we ask anything according to His will, He hears us. And if we know that He hears us—whatever we ask—we know that we have what we asked of Him.

So, he felt confident that if He continued to pray for a desire for God's Word that God would come through. Sure enough, after reading the New Testament consistently over a period of time out of obedience, God eventually answered his prayers and gave him an incredible hunger for God's Word. That young man is now one of the authors of this material!

Third, learn from those who are strong at studying and teaching the Word. The Christian life was never meant to be a solo effort. God has uniquely led some of His people to devote their lives to study, interpret and apply God's Word.

And the things you have heard me say in the presence of many witnesses entrust to reliable people who will also be qualified to teach others. (II Timothy 2:2)

It was He who gave some to be apostles, some to be prophets, some to be evangelists, and some to be pastors and teachers, to prepare God's people for works of service, so that the body of Christ may be built up until we all reach unity in the faith and in the knowledge of the Son of God and become mature, attaining to the whole measure of the fullness of Christ. (Ephesians 4:11-13)

In a large gathering of believers you can worship together with others and hear the teaching of a mature student of the Bible. In small groups, you can discuss the meaning and implications of Scriptures. Getting involved in a dynamic, Bible-believing local church will both motivate you to keep up your personal Bible study and keep you on track with your understanding of Scripture.

And let us consider how we may spur one another on toward love and good deeds. Let us not give up meeting together, as some are in the habit of doing, but let us encourage one another—and all the more as you see the Day approaching. (Hebrews 10:24,25)

In the introduction, we talked about the model airplanes and instruction guides. Follow God's instruction book and you'll avoid a lot of life's disasters.

End Notes:

(1) Nelson Glueck, *Rivers in the Desert: History of Negev* (Philadelphia, PA: Jewish Publications Society of America, 1969), 31.

(2) Cited from Dr. Henry F. Schaefer, III, *Scientists and Their Gods*, http://leaderu.com/offices/schaefer/docs/scientists.html (2001).

(3) Frederick Copleston SJ, *A History of Philosophy Volume 1: Greece & Rome from the Pre-Socratics to Plotinus, Part 1* (New York, NY: Doubleday, 1993), 7.

(4) Frederick Copleston SJ, *Memoirs of a Philosopher* (Kansas City, MO: Sheed and Ward, 1993), 44.

(5) Josh McDowell, *Evidence That Demands a Verdict*, Volume 1 (San Bernardino, CA: Here's Life Publishers, 1979), 17.

The Bible
The Word Of God

Important to Leader: Answers and notes to leaders are in gray, italicized text.

GOAL:

For the disciple to begin to be acquainted with the structure of the Bible and to appreciate its uniqueness.

GETTING STARTED:

Why do you think that year after year the Bible is listed on the NY Times bestseller's list?

Transition: *Let's look at some of the things that make the Bible unique.*

STUDYING TOGETHER:

Read II Timothy 3:16.

1. What three things do we learn from this verse about Scripture?

   a) It originates with God ("God breathed"). b) It is useful for teaching, rebuking and training in righteousness. c) It equips Christians for good works.

2. What do you think training in righteousness means?

   Learning right from wrong. Learning the practical aspects of how to walk with God.

3. Some other purposes of the Bible are found in the following verses. Please look them up and summarize what some of the purposes of the Bible are.

   NOTE: *New believers may only be able to answer using words that are in the biblical text. You need to help them understand the **concepts** listed in the answers.*

   Psalm 103:8-12

   These verses tell us about God's character.

   I Peter 3:18a

   This verse tells us about God's plan of salvation.

Acts 17:26-27

These verses tell about God's long-term plan for this world and His people.

4. Read the Arrangement portion of the Exhibit "Arrangement And Uniqueness Of The Bible." (Exhibit is at the end of this lesson.)

   NOTE: *After locating and reading the Arrangement portion of the Exhibit, ask students to open their Bibles to the Table of Contents and show them the arrangement and chronology of the Old Testament and New Testament.*

5. Read the "Uniqueness" portion of the Exhibit. The Bible retains its harmony and unity throughout. What is the implication of this?

   Someone (God) coordinated the writing and assembling of the Bible. There is no other writing like Scripture. This is miraculous!

Read II Peter 1:20-21.

6. What does the Bible give as the reason for its uniqueness?

   The Holy Spirit guided the whole process.

Read Psalm 19:7-11.

7. How does the Psalmist describe the Word?

   It is: without error, trustworthy, instructive, valuable (more precious than gold and sweeter than honey), desirable, protective, gives joy, etc.

LOOKING AT REAL LIFE:

Read Psalm 1:1-3.

8. According to these verses, what are some of the benefits of the Word to a Christian?

   If a Christian loves the Word and meditates on it, he will be blessed. He will grow. His faith will be strong especially in difficult times. The Word will sustain him in hard times. It will make him fruitful (that is, it will make him have an impact for God's kingdom).

9. What are some of the ways we can gain more understanding about the Bible?

    Reading the Bible, being in a Bible study, going to church and listening to sermons; asking the Holy Spirit to reveal truth.

10. What hinders Christians from gaining more understanding of the Bible?

    Laziness, lack of planning and priorities, ignorance, distractions from life, etc.

LOOKING AT MY LIFE:

Which of the ways mentioned above (question #9) are you engaged in?

Which areas would you like to add to what you are presently doing?

What in your life is likely to hinder you from growing in your understanding of the Bible?

What can you do to deal with these hindrances (in question above)?

IMPORTANT NOTE: A good place to start reading the Bible is with the book of Mark in the Gospels.

Arrangement And Uniqueness Of The Bible

ARRANGEMENT OF BOOKS

Old Testament—Four Parts

1. Law—The first five books that God gave to Israel (Genesis–Deuteronomy) Also contains the early history of the world and Israel.
2. History—Twelve books that give the history of God's dealings with Israel (Joshua–Esther)
3. Poetry—Five books of poetry (Job–Song of Solomon)
4. Prophecy
   a. Five major (long) prophets (Isaiah–Daniel)
   b. Twelve minor (short) prophets (Hosea–Malachi)

New Testament—Four Parts

1. The four Gospels—Four different authors write about Jesus' life.
2. Acts—Luke writes a history of the early church.
3. Epistles
   a. There are thirteen letters written by Paul (Romans–Philemon).
   b. There are eight general epistles written by five different authors (Hebrews–Jude).
4. Revelation—John writes a final apocalyptic, highly symbolic and prophetic letter about the end of the world and the second coming of Christ.

Chronology in the Bible

1. Old Testament: First five books and the history books are in chronological order. The remainder of the Old Testament books fit within the chronology of the history books.
2. New Testament: The four Gospels chronologically come before Acts and the epistles. A number of the epistles fit back into the chronology of Acts. Revelation is the last book of the Bible.

UNIQUENESS OF THE BIBLE

There was great diversity in the way the Bible came into being.

1. It consists of 66 books—39 in the Old Testament and 27 in the New Testament.
2. It was written over a span of 1600 years.
3. It was composed by 40 different authors.
4. It was written by men from all walks of life, under different conditions, on three different continents, in three languages, concerning hundreds of controversial subjects.

In spite of the incredibly diverse ways it came into being, the Bible retains its harmony and unity throughout.

Prayer
Communicating With God

I recently saw news footage of a famous actor filming in a small Wisconsin town. The sidewalks were filled with adoring fans who had traveled for hours to stand and watch, dreaming of an opportunity for a handshake and autograph, but content with just a glimpse of their cinematic hero.

For a moment, imagine yourself as one of these fans, standing on a frigid Wisconsin sidewalk, hoping for a sighting. Suddenly, a limo pulls up beside you and the actor himself steps out, shakes your hand, and offers you a ride! "I'm a bit lonely today," he explains. "Being hours away from any friends or family, I asked around for some friendly locals who might be fun to hang out with. Your name kept coming up. Hey, I've got the day off from filming. Would you have time to show me around, chat a bit, and introduce me to your friends?"

Imagine the awe, the amazement, the disbelief, that a person of such stature would want to spend time with a regular person—you!

Some of the same feelings and concerns should flood over us when we realize that the Creator of the universe desires to talk and spend time with us. "God wants to hang out with me? Cool! But surely I'll be rather boring to One so great. And maybe He won't like me if we get too close. He'll see all my faults. And what in the world do you say to a Person like that?"

Keep those thoughts in mind as we look to God's Word for answers.

"ME? RELATING TO HIM?" BREAKING DOWN THE BARRIERS.

God's so far above us in every way. He's strong; we're weak. He knows all; we see bits and pieces. He's perfect; we're imperfect. How can we relate to a God like that?

First, God assures us that He loves us, no matter how far short we fall.

For God so loved the world….(John 3:16a)

Second, God destroyed the barrier that separated us. We are sinners, and God is holy. That is a barrier to our relationship.

…for all have sinned and fall short of the glory of God…. (Romans 3:23)

For the wages of sin is death…. (Romans 6:23a)

So God wants to relate to us, but we've rebelled by going our own way. Even if we came back, we'd be sinful people trying to approach a holy God. Something had to give. God gave. He sent His only Son to die for our sins, so that we would no longer have to be separated from Him.

For Christ died for sins once for all, the righteous for the unrighteous, to bring you to God. (I Peter 3:18)

For those of us who have turned from our old rebellious life and accepted God's gift of salvation, we've gone from being dead in our sins to being alive to God (Romans 6:11; Ephesians 2:1-5). The sin barrier has been broken! Now we can approach God, not on the basis of our own merits, but on the merits of Jesus. We could never be cool enough to spend time with God. But because Jesus cleansed us with His blood, we can approach His throne in clean, white robes. Because of Jesus, we can have a relationship—a friendship with God!

> Like any relationship, our friendship with God grows through communication.

Like any relationship, our friendship with God grows through communication. That's what prayer is all about—talking to God and listening to Him. Here are some practical hints to a more meaningful prayer life.

HINTS FOR TALKING TO GOD

1. Speak naturally.

God isn't impressed with memorized formulas, lots of words, or religious language (Matthew 6:7,8). You've probably heard people pray like this: *"I pray Thee, O Father, that Thou bless Thy child Mike, who has wandered from Thy paths."*

Don't worry. Jesus never said that He preferred prayers like that. It's your heart that counts, so use the words that best express your heart. My translation of the above prayer might be, "God, could you please help Mike? He's in trouble and really needs Your help."

2. Use variety.

For some people, every prayer is asking God for something. What if you had a friend whose only conversation involved asking you for things? That relationship's not going anywhere. Broaden your communication with God by including different aspects of prayer. I'll put them in a handy acrostic *(P.R.A.Y.)* to help you remember:

*P*raise Him: *"I love you God!"* Thank Him for who He is and what He has done for you. Be creative! Walk a field and thank Him for all you see. Write a list of things you've never thanked Him for (like the moisture in your eyes that keeps them from hurting). Sing Him a song. Write Him a poem. Worship Him both privately and with others. Since He is worthy of our worship (John 4:23-24), let's praise Him (I Thessalonians 5:18; Psalm 100, Psalm 150).

*R*equest Things: *"Lord, help me and others in need."* It's not selfish to pray for ourselves. God delights in our prayers and wants us to depend upon Him to meet our needs (Matthew 7:7-11; I Peter 5:7; Philippians 4:6,7).

But it's not all about us. Pray for others with needs, often greater than our own, both near and far away. God's given His children access to His awesome power that can transform the world. Since we're talking to the almighty God, don't hesitate to pray big (Colossians 1:9-12; Ephesians 1:15-23).

> It's your heart that counts, so use the words that best express your heart.

George Mueller's diary contains so many instances of answered prayer that, were it possible, a person could be bored by the miraculous. His heart was stirred by the plight of England's orphans in the mid-1800s. Seven-year olds worked 12 hours a day in factories. Escapees lived on the streets as thieves. Mueller, though a poor man himself, determined to build and operate an orphanage by faith and prayer alone, asking no person for financial assistance, telling no person of his financial needs, and never buying on credit.

By faith alone, Mueller eventually operated five orphan houses caring for 2,000 orphans! When money ran out or emergencies arose, the money always came, so that their needs were always supplied. For example, "in the two years, August 1838 to August 1840, there were fifty occasions on which they were either penniless, or had insufficient means to pay their way for the day. But the money always came." [1]

One morning Mueller had neither bread nor money to buy bread for the orphans. Rather than despair, he sat the orphans at the table and instructed them to bless their food. "What food?" the orphans must have thought. But they went ahead with the prayer. Just then, a knock came at the door. A bread truck had broken down nearby and the driver wished to donate the bread to the orphanage!

*A*dmit Your Sins: *"I'm sorry God."*

Confession is simply agreeing with God that you've sinned (I John 1:8,9). But since we learn to justify our behavior, it's hard for some of us to admit our shortcomings.

One day pastor Bill Hybels counseled a man ("Harry") who didn't see himself as sinful. Hybels knew him as a man he could shoot straight with, so he probed with a few questions.

"Have you been absolutely one hundred percent faithful to your wife...?"

"Well, you know, I'm in sales. I travel a lot...."

When Hybels asked about his business expense account, Harry admitted that he included things that weren't strictly his sales techniques; Harry admitted that he sometimes exaggerated. "That's the industry standard," he explained.

> We rationalize, minimize and cover up our sins. But God knows our sins. Why not just admit them to Him?

Hybels looked him in the eye and said, "You have just told me that you are an adulterer, a cheater and a liar. Repeat those words after me—*I am an adulterer, a cheater and a liar.*" Harry was horrified. He didn't see himself that way at all. In his view, he'd just fallen into a little of this and a bit of that—no big deal. [2]

Harry's like a lot of us. We rationalize, minimize and cover up our sins. But God knows our sins. Why not just admit them to Him?

Yearn and Listen: *"Here's how I'm feeling. What do You think?"*

Sometimes words can't express what we're feeling. That's okay.

In the same way, the Spirit helps us in our weakness. We do not know what we ought to pray for, but the Spirit himself intercedes for us with groans that words cannot express. (Romans 8:26)

Just be there with Him. He understands.

Often God speaks to us in promptings rather than words. So sometimes we need to simply be quiet and listen. Let's take this aspect of prayer a little further.

HINTS ON LISTENING TO GOD

Don't you hate it when friends or family members want to talk, talk, talk, but never listen? A one-way relationship is always shallow and seldom satisfying. Yet, most Christians rarely, if ever, hear God speaking audibly, like in dreams or visions. Here are some ways that we normally hear from God.

1. The Bible—God's Word to Us.

There's no need for God to repeat to us audibly what He's already told us in His Word. By reading it each day, we discover His wisdom on relationships, work, lifestyle, spiritual life, and all the areas of life that count (Psalm 1:1-3).

If you've never read the Bible much, start with the Gospel of John, which takes you through Jesus' life. Set a goal of reading about a chapter a day. Then, make your way through the rest of the New Testament. Some read a Psalm and a Proverb each day. Others use a devotional book, like *The Purpose Driven Life*. Find something that works for you!

It may be difficult to understand at first, but hang in there! Pray daily that God will give you a hunger for His Word. Pray for insight. God's Spirit enlightens our hearts, helping us to understand and apply Scripture to our lives (I Corinthians 2:12).

Go ahead, accept His invitation and start a conversation that can grow richer for the rest of your life.

2. Other Believers.

Don't just trust one person, even if he sounds totally sure of himself! There is safety in "many advisors" (Proverbs 15:22), especially those who are wise and insightful (Proverbs 20:18).

Also learn under gifted preachers and teachers (Ephesians 4:11-13) who spend unusual amounts of time studying the Bible. You can hear them at church, Bible study groups, through reading their books and listening to their audio messages.

3. Life's Circumstances.

God often opens and closes doors with the situations He allows us to encounter (I Corinthians 16:8,9).

4. Directing our Thinking.

As we pray for direction, study His Word, consult other believers and consider our circumstances, God directs our thinking, giving us the mind of Christ to make wise decisions (I Corinthians 2:15-16).

HINTS ON PRAYING ALWAYS

Paul encouraged the Thessalonians to "pray continually" (I Thessalonians 5:17). How does that work?

I think of it like my relationship with my wife on a day off from work. Often, we stop to have an extended conversation. But most of the day, we just bounce thoughts off each other, say words of encouragement and gratefulness, ask for help with a project, etc. That's how it should be with God—like spending a day with your best friend.

Read some of the Psalms. They are often so conversational, expressing doubts, fears, disappointments, frustrations, excitement, joy—what's going on in your heart right now—the stuff of real life.

WRAPPING IT UP

Thinking back to the actor inviting you into his limo—isn't it incredible that the God of the Universe wants to hang out with us? Go ahead, accept His invitation and start a conversation that can grow richer for the rest of your life. He's here. He cares. And He really wants to be your Friend.

End Notes:

(1) Compiled by A.J. Rendle Short, *The Diary of George Mueller, Great Man of Prayer* (Grand Rapids, MI: Zondervan Publishing House, 1972).

(2) Bill Hybels, *Too Busy Not to Pray: Slowing Down to Be With God* (Downers Grove, IL: InterVarsity Press, 1988), 54,55.

Prayer
Communicating With God

Important to Leader: Answers and notes to leaders are in gray, italicized text.

GOAL:

For the disciple to progress in her understanding and practice of prayer.

GETTING STARTED:

What are some of the differences between just watching a person and talking with that person?

With watching you can only observe the person's action and physical make up. Sometimes it is hard to discern motives, attitudes, thinking processes by merely watching a person. The result of this is that you have a high probability of misunderstanding the person.

If you talk with the person, you will be able to understand more about why the person is doing what she does. Obviously, the best alternative is to watch and talk with the person.

Transition: *In a similar way, talking with God increases our understanding of His heart, motives, character, and plans. This also helps us interpret His actions.*

STUDYING TOGETHER:

Read Revelation 3:20.

1. What does this verse tell you about our relationship with God?

   God is the initiator and desires fellowship with us, but He waits for us to respond and doesn't force His way in. He wants to spend time and interact with us.

Read Hebrews 4:15-16.

2. According to these verses, why can we have the confidence to approach God?

   We can approach God with confidence because Jesus understands our struggle and promises to give us grace and mercy when we need them.

Read Psalm 103:1-4 (NIV version); I John 1:9; I Thessalonians 5:18; Philippians 4:6-7; Ephesians 6:18.

3. According to the verses above, what should we communicate with God (talk with Him) about?

   Suggestion to Leader: *You may want to assign these verses, 1 per person (or if group is large, 1 verse per 2 or 3 people). Ask each person(s) to read the verse(s) and share the answer to question #3 with the group:*

   Psalm 103:1-4 (NIV version):

   We should praise God and tell Him what we appreciate about His character and thank Him for His works.

4. What are some ways we can praise God?

   Extol Him for His attributes (His love, His grace, His patience, etc.). Thank Him for His goodness to us. Thank Him for answers to prayer. Etc.

   I John 1:9:

   We should confess our sins.

5. Why do we need to confess our sins if God already knows about them and they have been forgiven?

   Confessing our sins makes us more aware of the ways we fail to please God. It is good for us to be reminded of God's forgiveness.

   I Thessalonians 5:18:

   We should give thanksgiving.

   Philippians 4:6-7:

   We should share our personal needs with God.

6. Isn't it selfish to ask God to meet our personal needs?

   God wants to meet our personal needs. It gives Him pleasure to meet our needs.

   Ephesians 6:18:

   We should pray for others.

7. Name some ways God speaks to us.

   Through the Bible, impressions from the Holy Spirit, through other believers, circumstances, prayer, etc,

Read II Timothy 3:16; Acts 13:1-3; Acts 8:29-35; Acts 8:1b,4; I Corinthians 2:12.

Suggestion to Leader: *You may want to assign these verses, 1 per person (or if group is large, 1 verse per 2 or 3 people). Ask each person(s) to read the verse(s) and share the answer to question #8 with the group:*

8. What does each verse(s) tell us about how God communicates with us?

   II Timothy 3:16:

   God communicates through Scripture, His Word.

   Acts 13:1-3:

   Communicates through the Holy Spirit.

   Acts 8:1b,4:

   Communicates through circumstances, situations.

   Acts 8:29-35:

   Communicates through the Holy Spirit, scriptures, interaction with other believers.

   I Corinthians 2:12:

   Communicates through our own thoughts, under the influence of the Holy Spirit.

Read I Thessalonians 5:17.

9. What do you think it means to "pray continually"?

   Note to Leader: *Allow group members to give their thoughts.*
   You may want (need) to present the following information:
   "Obviously, no one prays continuously, so what does this mean? Think about it this way: Throughout the day, God is with us as our companion whom we can talk to at any moment. It is like spending the day with a best friend. We talk and listen to Him as the need or desire arises, just as we do when we spend time with a friend."

LOOKING AT REAL LIFE:

10. What are some of the similarities and the differences between talking with God and talking with another person?

11. Discuss how Jesus becoming human helped God communicate with us?

LOOKING AT MY LIFE:

What are the benefits to you of communicating (listening and talking) with God? What step will you take this week to improve your communication with God?

What ideas in this discussion were most helpful to you?

Fellowship Of Believers
The Gathering Of God's People

I hear people say, "I love God. I read His Word. But I don't see any good reason to go to church. I can be a good person without going to church. Besides, so many of those people are hypocrites!" What reasons do you hear from those who don't attend church? Do you think their reasons are legitimate?

Let's look to the New Testament to discover God's plan for the church, and how church could make a difference in our lives.

HOW IT ALL BEGAN

During His time on earth, Jesus trained his disciples (later called apostles) to carry on His ministry and establish His church (Mark 3:14; Matthew 16:18). After Jesus' death, the apostles led the first church in Jerusalem, but eventually went out establishing churches everywhere, turning the leadership over to qualified believers (Acts 6:1-7; I Timothy 3:1-13; Titus 1:5-9).

SO, WHAT'S A CHURCH?

The Greek word for church, ekklesia, means "gathering." It's a gathering of believers who are committed to following God, ministering to one another and taking the message of God's love to the world.

In one sense, it's an organization, structured with regular meetings (Acts 20:7; I Corinthians 16:2) and official leaders (I Timothy 3:1-13). In another sense, it's an organism. Believers are members of God's family (Ephesians 2:19), so that we are spiritual brothers and sisters (Luke 8:21). Through this gathering, we draw closer to both God and other believers.

For where two or three come together in my name, there am I with them. (Matthew 18:20)

From Him (Christ) the whole body, joined and held together by every supporting ligament, grows and builds itself up in love, as each part does its work. (Ephesians 4:16)

Some might object, "But can't we draw closer to God simply through walking in the woods and draw strength from other believers by visiting at a coffee shop?" Sure. But for some reason the church gathering makes this happen in special ways that other methods can't. Perhaps that's why Hebrews challenges us:

> Once you establish a set of solid relationships, you've found a sweet fellowship that can change your life.

Let us not give up meeting together, as some are in the habit of doing.... (Hebrews 10:25)

WHAT THE CHURCH IS NOT: A GATHERING OF PERFECT PEOPLE

At a typical church service you'll find some dedicated believers who came to worship, others who came to please a spouse or parent, others who came to make business contacts, and still others who came to find someone to date. Even the committed believers aren't perfect (I John 1:8). Some are more mature than others. Some have better people skills than others. Some are downright obnoxious.

> God wired us to function best in the context of significant relationships. We need each other.

Since we don't know people's hearts or their private lives, it's often hard to tell the sincere from the insincere. So don't get turned off when you meet hypocrites at church. We should expect them! Even one of Jesus' original twelve disciples was a hypocrite: Judas. But once you establish a set of solid relationships, you've found a sweet fellowship that can change your life.

Here are a few of the reasons that God wants us to get involved with a local church.

1. For Fellowship

God wired us to function best in the context of significant relationships. We need each other. Successful individuals have often discovered the value of regularly hanging out with those who have similar interests and goals.

Twenty-two-year-old Albert Einstein and likeminded friends met frequently in each other's homes and talked on hikes, sometimes all the way through the night. These conversations had an enormous impact on his future work. They called themselves "The Olympia Academy."

Fifteen-year-old Bill Gates met regularly with other computer enthusiasts who called themselves "The Lakeside Programmers Group."

Benjamin Franklin met every Friday for decades with a diverse group of civic-minded thinkers called "Junto." Many of his great accomplishments were a result of cross-pollination from this group.

Writers J.R.R. Tolkien and C.S. Lewis met with a group called "The Inklings," on a weekday morning and Thursday evenings at Lewis' house, often reading their manuscripts aloud to get input. I think it's significant that the groups were organized enough to have names: "The Inklings," "Junto," "The Lakeside Programmers Group," "The Olympia Academy."

If the synergy of such gatherings can make people vocationally successful, doesn't it make sense that regular gatherings with committed believers could make us spiritually successful? So what is it about fellowship that helps us spiritually thrive?

WHAT'S IN IT FOR ME?

First, fellowship stimulates us through the sharing of ideas (Hebrews 10:24,25). These extremely successful people found that the collaboration of several minds produces more wisdom than the sum of their thoughts working separately. It's the same in our spiritual lives. When I read the Bible on my own, I come up with a few applications to life. But when I study it with others, I discover a whole array of life applications that I would have never come up with on my own.

> Our spiritual fire will diminish if we forsake meeting with motivated believers.

Second, fellowship keeps us balanced in our thinking and our lifestyle (Ephesians 4:11-16). On our own, we gravitate toward certain teachings while ignoring others. I suppose that's why the New Testament authors had to spend so much time warning believers that they'd gotten off course with their understanding of grace or legalism or spiritual gifts or the second coming. Each believer offers wonderfully unique insights into Scripture and life that keep us out of spiritual ruts and guard us from extremes.

Third, we build relationships that motivate us spiritually. Close together, the sticks in your campfire burn brightly. Spread them out and the fire quickly goes out. In the same way, our spiritual fire will diminish if we forsake meeting with motivated believers.

And let us consider how we may spur one another on toward love and good deeds. Let us not give up meeting together, as some are in the habit of doing, but let us encourage one another—and all the more as you see the Day approaching. (Hebrews 10:24,25)

Fourth, we find support and encouragement for difficult times (I Thessalonians 5:11-15; II Corinthians 1:3,4). When my wife was ill with cancer, church folks brought meals and offered other practical help. Raising four boys, working, and caring for my wife overwhelmed me. I needed help. The church came through. But those relationships don't generally come from just having your name on a church role and showing up at Easter. It comes from developing solid relationships through participating in small groups, learning and serving together.

WHAT'S IN IT FOR OTHERS?

Fellowship isn't all about me. It's also about helping others. God's equipped each of us in special ways to build up, encourage and instruct others. You may not think you have much to offer. But God's Word says that each of us has been given gifts that are critical for the health of the church.

Each one should use whatever gift he has received to serve others....(I Peter 4:10)

"But I don't know what my gift is. How can I serve?" you might ask. I'd suggest, "Start serving wherever you see needs." Spend time with the lonely, encourage the discouraged, give advice to those needing counsel, keep the nursery, assist in a small group, help with clean-up, build wheelchair ramps for the needy...well, you get the idea.

There are many gifts and ministries (Romans 12:3-8; I Corinthians 12:1-31; Ephesians 4:11-16; I Peter 4:7-11), so start trying them out! The more I serve, the more I discover what ministries I enjoy, what people say I'm good at, what I'm most motivated and equipped to do. Ask the leaders of the church you attend to help you find areas of service that are appropriate for you.

And don't get infatuated with the gifts that get the most attention, like preaching and singing. The Apostle Paul likens the church to a body (I Corinthians 12:12ff.), with each part doing its part to make the body work. Toes and thumbs may not be glamorous, but if you wake up one morning to find them not working, you'll realize pretty quickly how important they are!

In other words, there are no small gifts. So take what you've got and begin serving.

2. For Learning the Word of God

We've just seen how the church is a family that nurtures us. But it's also a school that teaches us. Sure, I can read the Bible on my own. And I should (I Peter 2:2,3). As the Psalmist said,

Oh, how I love your law! I meditate on it all day long. (Psalm 119:97)

But I also learn from gifted teachers and preachers (Ephesians 4:11-13) who've spent years studying the Bible. While a young believer can read a chapter and glean some truth, a mature, gifted teacher can bring in many other related passages to bring balance and depth to that truth.

But just because teachers are gifted doesn't mean that they're infallible. That's why Luke praises the noble character of the Bereans. When Paul taught them, they didn't blindly follow. Instead, they "examined the Scriptures every day to see if what Paul said was true." (Acts 17:11) Over time, the nurture and teaching of the church helps us to grow up in our faith, so that we may one day find ourselves teaching others (II Timothy 2:2).

3. For Worship

What is Worship?

Worship is declaring God's worth—that He is above all else, number one in our lives, the One most worthy of our worship (I Peter 2:9). Someone has defined worship as "setting our mind's attention and our heart's affection on God, praising Him for who He is and what He has done."

> Worship is declaring God's worth—that He is above all else, number one in our lives, the One most worthy of our worship.

If that's true, then it's entirely possible to attend a worship service, but never truly worship! If we're more excited about our things and our friends than our God; if we sing songs about God while our thoughts are elsewhere, we're not really worshipping.

Why Worship?

First, God is worthy of our worship. He created this vast universe and breathed life into each of us. He sculpted the mountains, filled the oceans with water and created exquisite beauty with His masterful artistry. He provides rain and sunshine to grow our crops, His Word to light our path, intelligence and wisdom to navigate life.

And even after we failed Him horribly, rebelling and going our own way, He sent His Son to pay our penalty, so that we could experience true life and look forward to an eternity in heaven. Truly, God is worthy of our worship!

A second reason to worship is that it meets one of our deepest needs. Everyone worships something. If we fail to worship God, we'll find something else to worship, like material things, sex, power or false gods (Romans 1:21-23). But all those objects of worship fail miserably, leaving us feeling shallow and unfulfilled. God is the only object of worship who truly satisfies our deepest longings.

HOW TO WORSHIP

There are many ways to worship God, so don't get stuck in a rut! In the Bible, we find worshippers speaking, singing, and playing instruments to God. They used a variety of instruments (horns, cymbals, tambourines, stringed instruments) and praised Him in different locations (in a house, in nature, in His sanctuary, in bed, in jail), in different manners (leaping, clapping, dancing, lifting hands), with different content (thanking Him for personal blessings, for His character and attributes, for His creation).

Some people enjoy reading a Psalm to God; others write a letter of thanks to Him. Some sing to Him; others take a walk with Him, thanking Him for the beauty and wonder of their surroundings. Find what works best to keep your mind's attention and heart's affection focused on Him.

Often we worship privately, but neglect corporate worship in the gathering of believers (Colossians 3:15,16). "But can't I worship God just as well in the privacy of my bedroom, or in my car on the way to work? Why commute to worship when I can do it at home?"

Perhaps the best way to answer that question is to compare our relationship with God to our closest human relationships. Are you familiar with the concept of "love languages"? In brief, when I want to express my love for my wife, I don't express it in the ways that mean the most to me. I express love in the ways that mean the most to her—in her love language.

So if I love cold orange juice in the morning and she prefers hot coffee, what do I bring her in the morning to express my love? Obviously, the hot coffee. I don't have to like hot coffee. I don't have to understand why she likes hot coffee. It's enough that she told me that she likes coffee, likes it hot, likes it with a spoonful of sugar, and likes it in the morning. If I want to express love to my wife and her love language involves hot coffee, I will bring her coffee just as she likes it.

I think of worship in the same way. Some may think, "I don't like lots of people talking to me at the same time. I prefer intimate, one-on-one settings. God's probably the same way, preferring my individual worship more than group worship. Therefore I don't need to go to church to worship."

But if worship is about showing God our love for Him, we'd best pay attention to His love language more than our own. How does He tell that He prefers to be worshipped? Since we know that He established the church, called it His body, and that we see corporate worship demonstrated throughout the pages of Scripture, we have to assume that corporate worship is an important part of God's love language.

Praise the LORD. Sing to the LORD a new song, His praise in the assembly of the saints. (Psalm 149:1)

64

Finally, we worship God by the way we live. He's not impressed with beautiful voices, lengthy prayers or perfect church attendance on Sunday, if our hearts and actions are far from Him on Monday through Saturday.

And whatever you do, whether in word or deed, do it all in the name of the Lord Jesus, giving thanks to God the Father through Him. (Colossians 3:17)

WRAPPING IT UP AND APPLYING IT TO LIFE

Church isn't a place that we passively attend. It's a living fellowship where we actively interact with fellow believers and with God. All believers should find a church where they can have fellowship through building relationships, learning God's Word and worshipping Him.

If you're not currently involved with a church, make plans to visit a church with a friend this week. Perhaps the person who shared this Pocket Principle™ can recommend one. If you already attend a church, make sure you're deepening your relationships, learning His Word and truly worshipping.

To get more involved, consider praying these three things on the way to church,

"God, today at church, help me to:

- Meet other believers and encourage someone who might need help.

- Learn something from You and other believers that I can apply to my life.

- Truly worship You, rather than just say words while my mind is elsewhere."

If you want to express love to God in His love language, make church a part of your worship experience.

7 Fellowship Of Believers
The Gathering Of God's People

Important to Leader: Answers and notes to leaders are in gray, italicized text.

GOAL:

For the disciple to be encouraged to become involved in a local church.

GETTING STARTED:

What can happen to a person who becomes too isolated from others? (E.g. a hermit)

Out of touch with world events, with new inventions. Psychological problems may also occur, such as having a vivid fantasy life, depression, loneliness, ignoring own personal needs, rejecting relationships, having irrational fears, denying reality, denying need for help.

Transition: Although the effects are not necessarily as severe, a Christian suffers when he isolates himself from the fellowship of believers.

STUDYING TOGETHER:

Read I Corinthians 1:2.

1. In this verse Paul refers to the "church in Corinth." How does he describe the church?

    Composed of people who have been sanctified (set apart for holy purposes) in Christ Jesus and called to be holy. Everyone in the world who is a believer is a part of the church as a whole. The church is divided into many local groups that meet together regularly. On one level, the church is an organization, but on another more fundamental level, it is an organism.

2. In what ways is the church an organization? In what ways is it an organism?

    Organization: It has a schedule of meetings, an organizational structure (leaders, followers, etc.), and has a division of responsibility to carry out its purpose. Organism: It grows and matures (is called the Body of Christ). It's relational. God directs it. It has an influence in the world.

Read I Thessalonians 5:11-15. (This passage is addressed to the people in the church at Thessalonica.)

3.   What are some of the things Paul says for them to do in this passage?

Encourage one another, build each other up, respect their leaders, live in peace with each other, be patient with people, help the weak and misguided, be kind to people.

Read Hebrews 10:24-25.

4.   Describe the concern that the author of Hebrews had about church members.

That they would stop meeting together, stop encouraging each other. He warned them because he saw judgment (hard times) coming.

5.   How does this admonition relate to the church today?

Don't get lazy, complacent or discouraged. Keep meeting with each other for mutual encouragement because we do face hard times.

6.   Describe how interacting with believers inspires people to love and good works?

Read Ephesians 4:16.

7.   How does this verse say the church is suppose to operate?

Paul refers to the church as a "body," and to each of us as a part of that body. Each person needs to contribute to the growth of the body (church). The body suffers if each member doesn't do its part, and each part suffers if it's not involved with the rest of the body.

Read Acts 19:8-10, 20:26-27.

8.   What did Paul do that caused the church at Ephesus to become mature and have an effective ministry in the whole region?

He taught the Ephesians the Word of God (full counsel of God) for over two years (on a daily basis). He taught them everything they needed to know God, grow spiritually and reach others for Christ.

9. What does this story about Paul's ministry say to the church today?

   Paul's ministry was a good example of a more mature believer teaching and helping younger believers apply the Word of God. This is a good model for the church today.

LOOKING AT REAL LIFE:

10. What are some of the benefits of belonging to a church (the body of Christ)?

    Build relationships with other Christians, learn about God's Word, personal support and encouragement, observes the Christian life modeled by more mature believers, have the opportunity to help others through service, learn how to work as a team.

11. How would you answer a believer who says, "I can experience God all by myself, I don't have to be in a church"?

12. Why do you think it's important to participate in a local church?

LOOKING AT MY LIFE:

- Answer if you are attending a church:

  In your own life, how have you experienced the benefits of meeting with other Christians?

    OR

- Answer if you are not attending a church:

  What is causing you to hesitate? You may want to visit a friend's church (or get a recommendation from a Christian you know and trust)

Future Growth

When my two sons were young we went to Atlanta for the groundbreaking of one of the more famous skyscrapers. We had been reading about the project for months in the local papers and were excited to watch the construction of the "tallest building in the South." As we arrived on the scene, the bulldozers were already clearing the site, but there was a viewing area for spectators with an architectural rendering of the completed structure emblazoned on the side of the construction fencing. "Wow!" my oldest exclaimed, "It's humongous!" And indeed it was, soaring nearly seventy stories above Peachtree Street, it certainly promised to be a focal point of the city skyline.

We faithfully trekked to the site and watched trucks haul away dirt and debris while other trucks delivered steel girders and other building materials. After several weeks of this vigil, one of the boys exclaimed in frustration, "Dad, when are they going to start working on the building?" (It was a question that I had pondered myself, because all that existed was a large hole and lots of mud.) Approaching a worker with a set of plans under his arm, I inquired, "Can you give us some idea when the building is going to begin?" His chuckle made it obvious the question had come up before.

"It's hard to believe it," he said, "but this hole is the most important part of the building. We have to dig down several hundred feet and build a solid foundation to support a structure that's over seventy stories tall. It will take several months to pour the concrete and sink the steel pillars, but then we'll start going up. Once we start, it will rise pretty fast!"

The success of our Christian walk is determined by the strength of our spiritual foundation.

The Bible compares living the Christian life with constructing a building. Just as there are phases in building a building, there are phases in the growth of a Christian, and the first phase is: "laying a foundation." Our initial salvation experience is the beginning of a process of growth that lasts a lifetime. The success of our Christian walk is determined by the strength of our spiritual foundation. Matthew 7:24-27 asserts that the Christian life built on a solid foundation will withstand the storms of life. The tallest building in the South is still standing today. Believers who lay solid foundations are more likely to stand tall than those who fail to establish a solid base for growth.

This foundations phase actually consists of four interconnecting parts: 1) relating to God, 2) relating to other Christians, 3) understanding truth, and 4) applying truth so that it transforms us. Let's explore these together!

RELATING TO GOD

Unlike other religions, the essence of Christianity is a relationship with God, not a set of rules. In John 17:3, the Scripture affirms that eternal life is all about knowing God. It is thrilling to remember that God desires a relationship with us that will never end. The great news is that believers don't have to wait for heaven to experience this. It begins the moment we accept Christ!

Having a relationship with God is not all that different from having a relationship with anyone else. As we relate to others, we get to know them better and the relationship deepens over time. There are specific situations that will help believers better experience a relationship with God. The first of these involves setting aside time for personal devotions, a quiet time each day devoted to prayer, Bible reading, and personal meditation. The Scripture promises in James 4:8 that as we come near to God, He will come near to us. This coming near to God is not a religious duty, but a time for relational development. Of course, just as good disciplines and habits can be beneficial in other areas of life, the more we remain faithfully committed to our quiet time, the more benefit we derive from it.

Unlike other religions, the essence of Christianity is a relationship with God, not a set of rules.

Another aspect of developing a relationship with God is attending public worship in a church that exalts Him. Although we can worship God any place, any time, worshipping with other Christians deepens and develops our ability to relate to God. There are many different public worship experiences and not all churches structure them in the same way.

Worship that focuses on the greatness of God and includes times of singing praise, prayerful meditation, and Biblical preaching should be a priority. Ask God to help you find a church in your community and become a part of the fellowship. This leads to another important part of laying a good foundation— relating to other Christians.

RELATING TO OTHER CHRISTIANS

God has placed us in His spiritual family, the Church, to encourage us, protect us, correct us, direct us, and provide for us. Again there are specific situations that help believers experience relationships with other Christians. Each of these plays a unique role in helping to form a spiritual foundation, and each will require some effort. But they all are incredibly beneficial. Christians who do not have connections with other Christians tend to stop growing (cf. Hebrews 10:24-25).

In the first century there were very few church buildings. Mostly the believers met together in private homes for Bible teaching, prayer, and fellowship. There are benefits to meeting with large groups in public worship, but there is also an advantage gained from being part of a small group. The intimacy of the setting provides a place for relationships to flourish. Many modern believers have learned that meeting together in small groups helps to forge close relationships as members discuss Scripture, pray for each other, and share personal matters.

The term "life coaching" was coined by the modern business community to describe a relationship where a seasoned executive tutors a younger colleague in commercial practices. But long before mentoring was introduced to the world of commerce, it had already existed in the spiritual community as "one-to-one discipleship." In this case, it describes an intentional relationship between a young believer and a more mature Christian who models the Christian life, answers questions, gives counsel, and helps the younger Christian stay focused on the priorities of growth.

UNDERSTANDING TRUTH

One important priority for growth (and the third part of laying good foundations) involves developing an increasing understanding of God's truth. The Bible is the Book of Truth for Christians, but it can appear overwhelming to a new learner. It was Jesus who proclaimed that knowing truth sets people free from the bondage of sin. Therefore, it is helpful to have a basic plan of study for learning the truths that we need to build upon, a plan that focuses on specific themes and principles of foundational development. A good beginning series of studies for young believers should include themes such as: truth that helps someone to know more about God, truth that helps people understand themselves, and truth that helps someone to grow spiritually.

Christians who do not have connections with other Christians tend to stop growing (Hebrews 10:24-25).

There are specific approaches to gaining an understanding of these foundational truths. This series you have just read is the first in a curriculum of systematic instruction. Next is a series called Laying Foundations, which is designed specifically for helping new believers (or mature believers wanting a review) lay solid spiritual foundations.

Another way of gaining insights into living the Christian life is by reading. There are many excellent materials and resources available in Christian bookstores, libraries, and on the Internet. Your own informal reading will supplement your growth. But be sure to focus on the foundational themes mentioned above as a starting point.

Your local church is also an excellent source of content. Besides the weekly sermon delivered by the pastor or other teacher, many churches offer small groups devoted to helping new believers get established in the faith. Consult the churches in your area for opportunities to learn foundational truths.

APPLYING TRUTH

But as important as truth is in the growth process, it is not the information alone that transforms us. In fact, other parts of Scripture warn us that knowledge by itself can be dangerous, leading to spiritual pride and the deadening of our hearts to God. This particular sin characterized the Pharisees who were enemies of Christ. It is only truth that is obeyed or applied to our lives that changes us and causes growth. Romans 12:2 reminds us that it is a life consecrated to obeying God that is impacted by truth. When our minds are transformed in this way we help establish the will of God on earth. This is more than just knowing the truth, it is actually doing truth.

> It is only truth that is obeyed or applied to our lives that changes us and causes growth.

A skyscraper is an engineering marvel, but soaring high means digging deep and laying solid foundations. A maxim of the Christian life asserts that "you can only grow as tall as you grow deep." Laying good foundations takes time and effort, but the benefits are worth it. The new believer needs to embrace experientially the truths related to knowing and understanding God and other believers.

CONCLUSION

Applying truth will require becoming involved in specific situations that facilitate foundational growth. Establishing a time for personal devotions, joining a small group, locating an older believer who can come alongside you as an encouraging mentor, setting up a systematic plan of study, and participating in public worship are layers of spiritual brick and mortar that form this foundation. But these situations without a heart commitment to obey the truth will not suffice. Blessings to you as you grow!

Future Growth

8

Important to Leader: *Answers and notes to leaders are in gray, italicized text.*

GOAL:

For the disciple to be motivated to take the next step in his spiritual growth.

GETTING STARTED:

What are some of the tasks a person needs to do to build a house?

Build foundation, floors, walls, electric and plumbing, HVAC, flooring, roof, windows, paint walls, finish the ceiling, etc.

What would the builder do first and why?

The foundation is laid first. It provides the stability and strength to hold the building upright.

Transition: *In the same way, many things help us grow spiritually, but a disciple must have a good foundation for those things.*

STUDYING TOGETHER:

Read Romans 8:15-16.

1. According to these verses, when you became a Christian, what new relationship began?

   A relationship with God: the Father, the Son and the Holy Spirit.

   Describe this new relationship.

   It is a close relationship like a family: God is the Father and we are his sons and daughters.

2. This passage uses the word "abba," which is an intimate term used by a child to address his father. It is similar to our word "daddy."

   What does the use of the term "abba" imply about our relationship with God?

   The relationship is intimate, personal, safe, open communication, honest, etc.

Read Psalm 95:1-2,6-7.

3. In these verses what does the Psalmist call us to do?

   To worship God by singing, shouting, etc. because of who He is and what He has done.

God has made us in such a way that we need to worship him as individuals and with other believers.

Read Hebrews 10:24-25.

4. What are some of the results of believers meeting together?

   People are encouraged to do good deeds. They are comforted in the midst of difficult times. People get some of their emotional needs met when believers meet.

Beyond the public worship service, there are two ways that Christians can encourage each other: in small groups and in individual meetings.

Read Acts 20:20-21,25-27.

5. Paul had spent 3 years in Ephesus teaching at the school of Tyrannus. He was now talking to the leaders of the church and recounting his time there. From the verses above, what was Paul trying to accomplish while he was there?

   He taught what was helpful to them; declared the Gospel to nonbelievers. For believers, he taught the whole counsel of God.

6. Why do you think Paul taught the content he did?

   He was teaching the elders, and since they would be leading/teaching others, they needed a good solid background.

7. How did he go about accomplishing these tasks?

   Publically: in worship services and classroom; house-to-house: in small groups and with individuals

Read John 8:31-32.

8. What is the great promise that Jesus gives us?

   His truth will set us free.

Free from what?

The bondage of the lies of this world (both religious and secular).

Is it enough to know what the Word says? *No*
Give a reason for your answer.

I must apply the truth in order to fully understand it.

LOOKING AT REAL LIFE:

9. Why do you think God wants to have a relationship with us?

10. What are some of the lies that the world tells us?

LOOKING AT MY LIFE

In your own life, what benefits have you experienced in the body of Christ (church, small group, etc.)?

Which of the world's lies do you believe or have you believed?

How has a relationship with God and other believers helped you identify these lies?

What's Next?

We hope you enjoyed this study.
You may be wondering: "So, what's next?"
I'm glad you asked.

If your group has benefited from their experience with this study, we suggest that you continue the Cornerstone series. The next group of studies in this series is entitled *Laying Foundations,* which includes *Knowing God* (10 studies), *Understanding People* (10 studies) and *Growing Spiritually* (10 studies.) All of these studies follow the same format as *Getting Started.* (See links on next page.)

Because you have chosen to lead, we want to do all we can to support you. In addition to the materials provided in this workbook, we would like to also offer you a free download of the Teaching Outlines for *Getting Started.*
(See link on next page.)

If you want to study materials that will help you grow as a leader, you might be interested in the *Small Groups Manual* (WDA) or the *Life Coaching Manual* (WDA), both can be found on the WDA store at www.disciplebuilding.org. (See link on next page.)

Also, **on the WDA website you will find explanations about the meaning of the different Phases I through V.** If you want to understand more about progressive growth there is a free download on our website called *Disciple Building: A Biblical Framework.* This explains the biblical basis for our disciple building process. (See links on next page.)

If you want to understand more about the Restorative Ministry, there is a free download entitled *How Emotional Problems Develop* on our website. The Restorative Ministry addresses relational and emotional needs that affect a disciple's ability to grow spiritually. (See links on next page.)

We look forward to a long association with you as you seek and follow our Lord, and grow in Christ using WDA Materials.

Bob Dukes

Links

Knowing God, Understanding People and *Growing Spiritually:*
www.disciplebuilding.org/product-category/laying-foundations-phase-2

Free Teaching Outlines for *Getting Started:*
www.disciplebuilding.org/materials/getting-started-teaching-outlines-free-download

Small Groups Manual and *Life Coaching Manual:*
www.disciplebuilding.org/materials/description_materials/4
www.disciplebuilding.org/product-category/leadership-manuals

Meaning of Phases I-V:
www.disciplebuilding.org/about/phases-of-christian-growth/2

Free Download of *Disciple Building: A Biblical Framework:*
www.disciplebuilding.org/store/leadership-manuals/disciple-building-a-biblical-framework

Free Download of *How Emotional Problems Develop:*
www.disciplebuilding.org/store/leadership-manuals/how-emotional-problems-develop

About the Restorative Ministry:
www.disciplebuilding.org/ministries/restorative-ministry

About WDA

WDA's mission is to serve the church worldwide by developing Christlike character in people and equipping them to disciple others according to the pattern Jesus used to train His disciples.

Organized as Worldwide Discipleship Association (WDA) in 1974, we are based in the United States and have ministries and partners throughout the world. WDA is a 501c(3) non-profit organization funded primarily by the tax-deductible gifts of those who share our commitment to biblical disciple building.

WDA is committed to intentional, progressive discipleship. We offer a flexible, transferable approach that is based on the ministry and methods of Jesus, the Master Disciple Builder. By studying Jesus' ministry, WDA discovered five phases of Christian growth. This Cornerstone series focuses on the first and second phases, Phase I: Establishing Faith (the *Getting Started* study comes in here) and Phase II: Laying Foundations (*Knowing God, Understanding People* and *Growing Spiritually*), which address the needs of a young believer or a more mature believer who wants a review of foundational Christian truths.

The remaining phases are: Phase III: Equipping for Ministry; Phase IV: Developing New Leaders and Phase V: Developing Mature Leaders.

For more information about WDA please visit our website: www.disciplebuilding.org.

If you are interested in seeing other WDA materials, please visit the WDA store: www.disciplebuilding.org/store.

WDA Partnerships

Help us build disciples worldwide.

You can help us fulfill the great commission by becoming a Worldwide Discipleship Association (WDA) partner. WDA's mission is to serve the church worldwide by developing Christlike character in people and equipping them to disciple others according to the pattern Jesus used to train His disciples.

Since our inception in 1974 our materials and processes have been used in more than 90 U.S. cities and in over **55 countries**. We have created **over a million direct discipleship impacts** and have conducted face-to-face **training to over 17,000 pastors and leaders** around the globe! **Your support of WDA is vital to the success of our mission.** We pledge to serve as faithful stewards of your generous gifts to the ministry.

www.disciplebuilding.org/give/wda-partnership

Become a Partner Today

Made in the USA
Columbia, SC
28 July 2019